Statistical Methods for Quality Improvement

Statistical Methods for Quality Improvement

Hitoshi Kume

THE ASSOCIATION FOR OVERSEAS TECHNICAL SCHOLARSHIP (AOTS)

Statistical Methods for Quality Improvement
First published in Japan 1985 by
3A Corporation
Shoei Bldg., 6-3, Sarugaku-cho 2-chome, Chiyoda-ku, Tokyo, 101

©The Association for Overseas Technical Scholarship 1985
AOTS
30-1, Senju-azuma 1-chome, Adachi-ku, Tokyo, 120

ISBN 4-906224-34-2 C0034

Reprinted with corrections April 1987
Reprinted September 1987
Reprinted August 1988
Reprinted March 1989
Reprinted June 1990
Reprinted May 1991
Reprinted January 1992

Printed in Japan

Contents

Preface

Statistical methods are effective tools for improving the production process and reducing its defects. However, you must keep in mind that statistical tools are just tools: they would not work, if used inadequately.

People often try to reduce production defects by tracing directly back to the cause of the defect. That is a straightforward approach and, at first glance, it seems to be efficient. But, in most cases, the causes obtained from that approach are not true ones. If remedies are taken for defects based on the knowledge of those false causes, the attempt may be abortive, the effort wasted. The first step in finding true cause is careful observation of the phenomenon of the defect. After such careful observation, true cause becomes apparent.

Statistical tools lend objectivity and accuracy to observation. The maxims of statistical way of thinking are:
1) Give greater importance to facts than abstract concepts.
2) Do not express facts in terms of senses or ideas. Use figures derived from specific observational results.
3) Observational results, accompanied as they are by error and variation, are part of a hidden whole. Finding that hidden whole is observation's ultimate goal.
4) Accept regular tendency which appears in a large number of observational results as reliable information.

One must first thoroughly understand imperfection of human recognition. One must then understand that knowledge presently held is nothing more than grounds for further hypotheses. After gaining that understanding, the above-mentioned methods of thinking can be used to further deepen our understanding of the production process and the ways to improve it.

This book differs from the ordinary textbooks on statistics. It aims to show how to apply the statistical methods to real world problems. Those with little knowledge of statistical analysis also stand to benefit. They should start with the initial steps of explanation and then move on to the other chapters. Persons already familiar with statistics can skip the introductory steps and go on to the explanations of statistical analysis in practical use.

The authors will be greatly pleased if the book aids plant managers and engineers in improving the production process.

The chapters are revised articles which first appeared in the quarterly *Kenshu*, published by The Association for Overseas Technical Scholarship (AOTS), a non-profit organization. AOTS's goal is promoting technical cooperation. *Kenshu*'s readers are plant managers and engineers of the developing countries. The chapters in the book and their authors are listed below, but responsibility for errors and omissions is the editor's.

Chapter 1	Introduction	Hitoshi Kume
Chapter 2	How to Obtain Data	Yoshinori Iizuka
Chapter 3	Pareto Analysis	Takenori Takahashi
Chapter 4	Cause-and-Effect Diagrams	Takenori Takahashi
Chapter 5	Histograms	Takenori Takahashi
Chapter 6	Scatter Diagrams	Masahiko Munechika
Chapter 7	Control Charts	Seijiro Oshimura
Chapter 8	Additivity of Variances	Hitoshi Kume
Chapter 9	Introduction to Statistical Inference	Yoshinori Iizuka
Chapter 10	The QC Story	Takenori Takahashi Hitoshi Kume
	Epilogue	Hitoshi Kume

My special thanks go to AOTS staff Iwao Ogawa, Nobutada Takebayashi (currently on loan to 3A Corporation) and Hideo Yoshihara for their hard work and enthusiasm in preparing this book for publication, and to John Loftus for his excellent translations of the original Japanese articles. Without their efforts, this book would still be merely a gleam in my eye.

Hitoshi Kume, *Editor*
July, 1985

Chapter *1*

Introduction

The Role of Statistical Methods in the Management of Production Processes

(1) What Causes Defectives?

One after another, products are arriving on the conveyor. At the end of the conveyor, there is a packaging machine which continuously packs up the incoming products and sends them to the product warehouse. A closer look reveals a man standing between the conveyor and the packaging machine. He is keeping a watchful eye on the flow of products, and occasionally picks up products and casually throws them into a basket behind him. Those products are defective.

This kind of thing is commonly seen in many factories. At first, those thrown-away products seemed to be waste of goods, but soon they are accepted as a routine process. But becoming accustomed to defectives does not solve the problem but is rather a step backward from the solution.

How are defectives made in the first place? What should be done to reduce their occurrence?

In order to decrease the number of defectives, one need to believe that defectives can definitely be reduced. Needless to say, belief alone cannot reduce the defectives. What we mean is that there are peculiar causes for any given defective product, and defectives can be got rid of if those causes are discovered and removed.

The way most people feel about defectives is that because their products must satisfy very strict quality standards and have numerous defect-causing factors, defective products are unavoidable.

However, regardless of types of product or kinds of production method used, causes of defectives are universal.

Variation: This is the cause. What will happen if we make products using materials of the exact same quality, identical machines and work methods and inspect these products in exactly the same manner? No matter how many products are made, they must all be identical as long as the above four conditions are identical. That is, the products will be either all conforming or all non-conforming . All of them will be defective if materials, machinery, method of work or that of inspection is not proper. In such a case, exactly identical defectives will invariably be produced. As long as there is no failure in the aforementioned four conditions, the resulting products must all be "identically" non-defective ones.

As far as the products we make are concerned, it is almost impossible that every product turns out to be defective. Of the products made, some are defective while others are not. In other words, defective and non-defective products come mixed together.

Why are defectives and non-defectives produced together? The cause, as we stated before, is variation. Variations in *materials,* in *machinery conditions,* in *work methods* and in *inspections* are the causes of defectives. If none of these variations existed, all products would be identical and there would be no varying of quality like the occurrence of defectives and non-defectives.

Let us consider the work of bending steel plates. All steel plates seem to have the same thickness. But when measured precisely, they will have different thicknesses. In addition, even within the same plate, some portions are thicker than others. If we go even further to inspect the crystal structure of the plates, there are slight variations in the shape of crystals made up of iron, carbon and other elements from one part of the plate to another. These differences naturally affect quality characteristics. Even when the same press method is employed, the plates will not be bent in a uniform way. Some of them may even develop cracks.

Next, let us look at machining. The cutting tool loses its sharpness as it processes a number of products. The condition of lubricating oil also changes with the change in temperature. Dimension of products varies with the way the cutting tool is set and positioned. Although it may seem that one operation is done under exactly the same condition as another, many changes or variations occur unnoticed, and they affect product quality.

Consider heat treatment as another example. Furnace temperature continuously changes with the change in voltage in the case of an electric furnace, and with changing gas pressure in the case of a gas furnace. In the furnace the area near the mouth, ceiling, floor or furnace wall and the central part, all have different conditions. When we put materials into the furnace for heat treatment, the amount of heat the materials receive varies according to the relative position of one material to another, affecting such quality characteristics as the hardness of the product.

Workers' physical characteristics and craftsmanship also affect products' quality variation. There are tall and short men, dexterous and clumsy ones, men with strong muscles and those who are weak, right-handed and left-handed persons. All workers may feel that they are working in the same way, but there are personal differences. Even a same individual works differently according to how he feels on each particular day and the condition of his tiredness. Sometimes he makes a very careless mistake.

In inspection, there may occur apparent variation in quality. If a gauge is used in an inspection, variation in data is caused by gauge disorder and the way in which the gauge is used. In the case of sensory inspections like visual inspection, quality appears to vary if there is a variation in the inspector's criteria. Variation in inspection has no direct relation to product quality variation itself, but affects the process of deciding whether a product is defective or not.

Looking at the problem in this manner, we can now see that in the process of making one product, there are countless factors which affect the quality characteristics of that product. When we regard manufacturing process from the viewpoint of quality variation, we can think of the process as *an aggregate of the causes of variation.* These causes are the explanation of the changes in quality characteristics of products, making defectives or non-defectives. A product is judged to be non-defective if its quality characteristics meet a certain standard and defective if they do not. Therefore, even non-defectives have variations within their standard. This means that these are not the "exactly equal" products which we discussed earlier.

Defectives are caused by variations. If these variations are reduced, defectives will certainly decrease. This is a simple, strong principle which holds true regardless of types of product or kinds of production method involved.

(2) Diagnosis of Processes

Although causes of quality variations are countless, not every cause affects quality to the same degree. Some of them actually affect quality greatly while others, although considered to be very important in theory, have very little effect on quality variation when they are properly controlled.

The countless conceivable causes can be categorized into two groups the first of which consists of a small number of causes which nevertheless give a great effect (the *vital few*) and a second group which is made up of many causes giving only minor effects (the *trivial many*). Usually, there are not many factors which really cause defects. This fact is called the *Principle of Pareto* because it applies to many instances.

By applying the aforementioned principle of variation and this Principle of Pareto, the problem of reducing defectives becomes considerably easier to tackle with. What we need to do first is to find the vital few causes of defectives, and remove these causes after they have been clearly identified. "In our process there are so many causes of defectives that it is really impossible to control them." This is the kind of comment one often hears from people involved in defective-ridden processes. Every process has many causes of quality variation, and it is not that any one process has an especially large number of such causes. There is a complete difference between having many "suspects" which might be causing defectives and really having many "culprits" which are actually causing defectives.

The procedure of finding the causes of defectives from among many other factors is called the *diagnosis of process*. In order to reduce the number of defectives, the first necessary action is to make a correct diagnosis to see what the true causes of defectives are. If this is not done correctly, defectives cannot be reduced. It is as if giving a binding medicine to an appendicitis patient, which does not cure him. The effect of the medicine might keep the patient better temporarily, but after a while the illness will come back in a worse form than before.

How do we make a correct diagnosis? There are various methods. Some employ intuition, others depend on experience. Still others involve statistical analyses on data, while one can also use experimental research. The intuititive method is often used because it can be done very quickly. In fact, there is something beyond ordinary man's ability in the intuition of the true expert, which must be given its due respect. A move that an expert chess player makes intuitively is superior to the move made by a band of a hundred amateurs. The advice and intuition of specialists and experts must be greatly respected. However, the difficulty in the problem of reducing defectives is that it is not always clear who a real expert is. In the case of chess,the advice of experts can be almost totally trusted because the stronger and the weaker are apparent in actual matches and champion players are those who have won and survived these tough matches. In the case of process diagnosis, however, often a seemingly good "physician" is not necessarily so but may turn out to be someone who "has left many patients to die." Moreover, in the time of rapid progress, it is difficult to remain an expert in all the problems whose nature is constantly undergoing change. As problems of defectives are often found in areas where previous experience is lacking, what is needed is not so much the years of experience as a strong will to reduce defectives and an attitude of observing the real situation in an objective way. The statistical way of looking at things and use of statistical methods are a most effective means for this observation.

Statistical methods provide a very effective means for the development of new technology and quality control in manufacturing processes. Many leading manufacturers have been striving for an active use of statistical methods and some of them spend more than 100 hours annually in in-company education of this subject. While knowledge of statistical methods is becoming part of the normal fixture of an engineer, the fact that one knows statistical methods does not immediately lead to the ability to use it. The ability to treat matters from the statistical viewpoint is more important than the individual methods. In addition, we need to be frank to recognize troubles and variation and to gather their data. Lastly, we want to emphasize that the important thing is not just the knowledge of statistical methods itself, but one's mental attitude toward using it.

Chapter **2**

How to Obtain Data

2.1 How to Collect Data

(1) Have Clear Defined Objectives

Data is a guide for our actions. From data we learn pertinent facts, and take appropriate actions based on such facts. Before collecting your data, it is important to determine what you are going to do with it.

In a machine factory, a sampling inspection was made on a certain type of incoming purchased part. A lot which should be rejected in itself was accepted as a special exception to keep the production schedule. However, they didn't do anything special about the accepted lot. This means that both the lots which conform to specifications and those which do not went to the next process. These data were certainly being taken to determine the acceptability of lots, but they were not utilized at all.

In quality control, objectives of collecting data are
1) Controlling and monitoring the production process,
2) Analysis of the non-conformance, and
3) Inspection.

Any data collecting has its own purpose and should be followed by actions.

(2) What Is Your Purpose?

Once the object for collecting data is defined, the types of comparison which need to be made are also determined, and this in turn identifies the type of data which should be gathered. For example, suppose there is a question involving variation in a quality characteristic of a product. If only one datum is gathered per day, it is impossible to determine the variation within a day. Or, if you want to know in what ways defectives are produced by two workers, it is necessary to take their samples separately so that the performance of each worker can be compared. If comparing one against the other reveals a clear difference, a remedial measure which will eliminate the difference between workers will also reduce the variation in the process.

Dividing a group in this way into several subgroups on the basis of certain factors is called *stratification*. Stratification is very important. It is necessary to make it a habit to apply stratification in your thinking in all kinds of situations.

Then, suppose you want to know the relationship between the amount of ingredient and the hardness of the product. In a case like this, where you want to know whether there is a relationship between the values of two characteristics, the data have to be available in pairs. If data are gathered in pairs, they can be analyzed using a *scatter diagram* which is explained in Chapter 6.

(3) Are Measurements Reliable?

Even if the samples have been taken properly, a wrong judgement will be made if the measurement itself is unreliable. For example, inspections made by a certain inspector showed a fraction defective which was very different from the rest, and careful examination later revealed that a measuring instrument had gone wrong.

In the case of a sensory measurement such as visual inpsection, differences due to individual inspectors are very common. This fact must be taken into account when collecting and analyzing data.

(4) Find Right Ways to Record Data

Once data is gathered, various statistical methods are used for analyzing them so that it will become a source of information. When collecting data, it is important to arrange it neatly to facilitate later processing. First of all, the origin of the data must be clearly recorded. Data whose origin is not clearly known becomes dead data. Quite often, little useful information is obtained despite the fact that a week was spent gathering data on quality characteristics, because people forgot on what days of the week the data was collected, which machines did the processing, who the workers were, which material lots were involved, and so on.

Secondly, data should be recorded in such a way that it can be used easily. Since data is often used later to calculate statistics such as means and ranges, it is better to write it down in a manner which will facilitate these computations. For example, data involving 100 pieces, obtained by making four measurements a day (at 9:00, 11:00, 2:00 and 4:00) for 25 days, should naturally be recorded on a data sheet, as shown in Table 2.1, on which time is arranged horizontally and days are listed vertically. In this way, daily computations can be done by checking the figures on each line, and those for the time can be done within each column. A set of standard recording forms should be prepared beforehand if data is to be collected on a continuous basis.

Table 2.1   An Example of a Data Sheet

Date	Time			
	9 a.m.	11 a.m.	2 p.m.	4 p.m.
Feb. 1	12.3	11.5	13.2	14.2
Feb. 2	13.2	12.5	14.0	14.0
Feb. 3	:	:	:	:

2.2   Check Sheets

As stated in the preceding section, if data is to be collected at all, it is essential to make the purpose clear and to have data which clearly reflects the facts. In addition to these premises, in actual situations it is important that the data should be gathered in a simple way and in an easy-to-use form. A *check sheet* is a paper form on which items to be checked have been printed already so that data can be collected easily and concisely. Its main purposes are two-fold:
1) To make data-gathering easy;
2) To arrange data automatically so that they can be used easily later on.

The collecting and recording of data seems easy but actually is difficult. Usually, the more people process the data, the more writing errors are likely to arise. Therefore, the check sheet, on which data can be recorded by means of check marks or simple symbols and on which data is arranged automatically without further copying by hand, becomes a powerful data recording tool. Followings are some examples of check sheets.

Example 2.1   Check sheet for production process distribution
Suppose we want to know the variation in the dimensions of a certain kind of parts whose machining specification is 8.300 ± 0.008. To study the distribution of process characteristic values, histograms are normally used. Such values as the mean and variance are computed

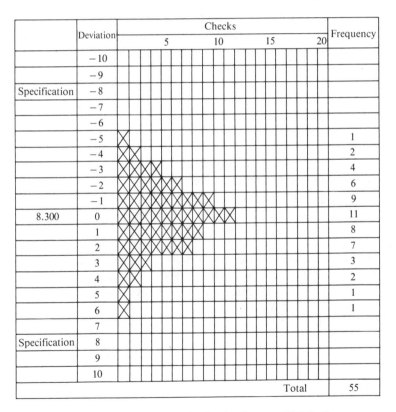

	Deviation	Checks 5	10	15	20	Frequency
	−10					
	−9					
Specification	−8					
	−7					
	−6					
	−5					1
	−4					2
	−3					4
	−2					6
	−1					9
8.300	0					11
	1					8
	2					7
	3					3
	4					2
	5					1
	6					1
	7					
Specification	8					
	9					
	10					
				Total		55

Figure 2.1   Check Sheet for Production Process Distribution

on the basis of the histogram and the shape of the distribution is also examined in various ways.

When making a histogram, it is doubly troublesome to collect a large number of data and then to make a graph showing a distribution of frequencies. A simpler way is to classify data exactly at the time of their collection. Figure 2.1 is an example of a form which can be prepared in advance. A cross is put in an appropriate box each time a measurement is made, so that a histogram is ready when the measurements are finished. When stratification is required and a single check sheet is used, it is better to use different colors or marks so that the difference will be recognizable later.

Example 2.2   Defective item check sheet

Figure 2.2 shows a check sheet used in the final inspection process of a certain molded plastic product. The inspector puts down a check mark every time he finds a defect. At the end of a day's work, he can immediately calculate the total number and types of the defects that occurred.

Merely knowing the total number of defects does not lead to remedial actions, but if a check sheet like this figure is used, very important clues can be obtained for process improvement because the data clearly shows which types of defect are frequent and which are not.

When using this check sheet, as was the case with Example 2.1, it will be impossible to stratify the data later, for instance, according to morning and afternoon, once they have been collected. Therefore, if stratification is judged to be necessary, this fact should be incorporated into the design from the beginning.

It is necessary to decide clearly beforehand how to record defects when two are found in a single product, and to give thorough instructions to the people who will do the tallying. In the case of Figure 2.2, 42 out of 1,525 pieces were defective. However, the total number of defects was 62 because sometimes two or more defects were found in a single piece.

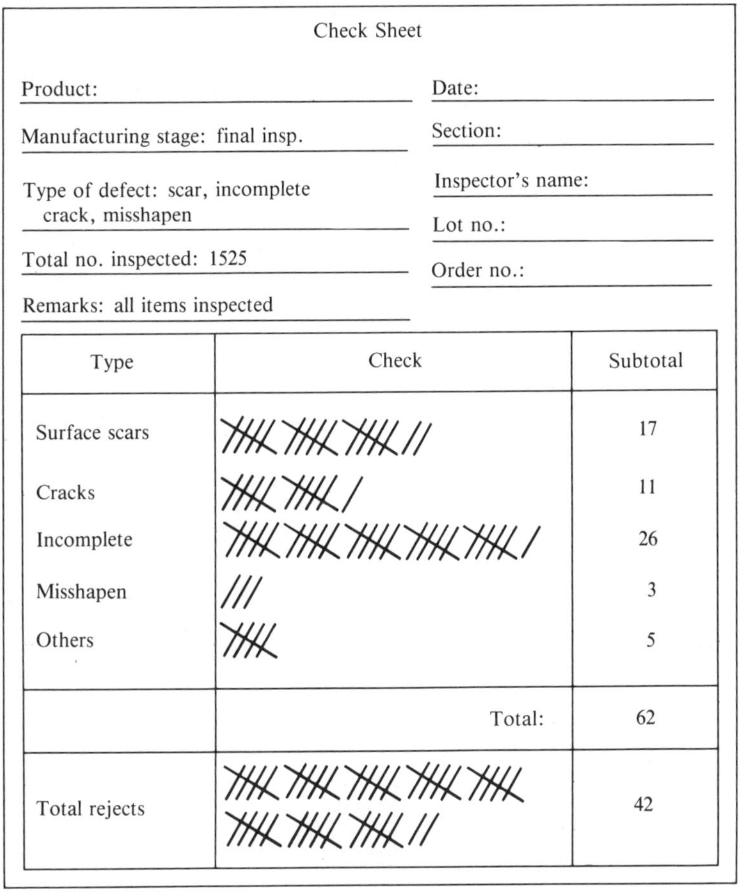

Check Sheet

Product: _____   Date: _____

Manufacturing stage: final insp. _____   Section: _____

Type of defect: scar, incomplete   Inspector's name: _____
  crack, misshapen _____   Lot no.: _____

Total no. inspected: 1525 _____   Order no.: _____

Remarks: all items inspected _____

Type	Check	Subtotal
Surface scars	卅 卅 卅 //	17
Cracks	卅 卅 /	11
Incomplete	卅 卅 卅 卅 卅 /	26
Misshapen	///	3
Others	卅	5
	Total:	62
Total rejects	卅 卅 卅 卅 卅 卅 卅 卅 //	42

Figure 2.2   Defective Item Check Sheet

Example 2.3   Defect location check sheet

External defects such as scratches and dirty spots are found on all kinds of product, and various efforts are being made at many plants to reduce this type of defect. The defect location check sheet plays a powerful role in solving this kind of problem. Generally, many check sheets of this type have sketches or expanded views on which markings are made so that the distribution of defect occurrence can be observed.

Figure 2.3 shows one such example used by a machine manufac-

14

Statistical Methods for Quality Improvement

turer for the acceptance inspection of their cast parts. The defect item is "casting blowhole," and previously the supplier was being informed only of the rejection or acceptance of each lot and the number of defects per lot. But quality did not show any improvement at all.

Blowhole Location Check Sheet

Product no. and name:

Material:

Maker:

1. Sketch

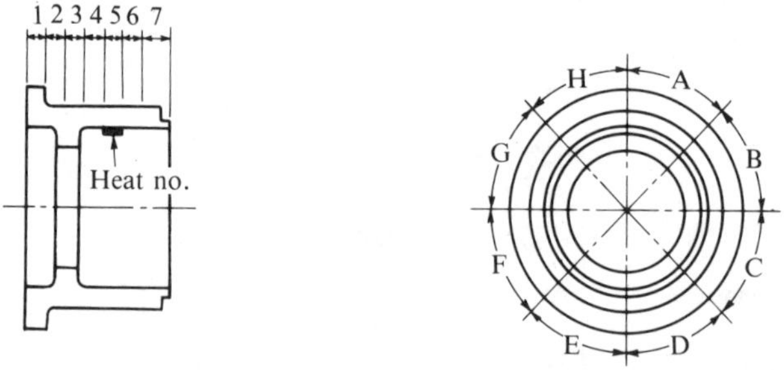

2. Defect location matrix

Circular \ Radial	1	2	3	4	5	6	7	10
A			/					▨1
B								
C								
D								
E	///		卌 /					▨▨▨ 9
F	/	//						▨ 3
G								
H								
10	▨ 4	▨ 2	▨ 7					13

Figure 2.3   Defect Location Check Sheet

After check sheets like the one in the figure were introduced, serving as inspection reports which even indicated where blowholes were likely to occur, quality improved greatly because finding the causes of defects became easier. This check sheet easily leads to action and is indispensable for process diagnosis, because the causes of defects can often be found by examining the places where defects occur and carefully observing the process to determine why defects become concentrated in these places.

Example 2.4   Defect cause check sheet

The check sheet in the preceding example is used for pinpointing location of defects. In addition, check sheets are sometimes used for further stratification in order to find the causes of defects. Generally speaking, most studies aimed at finding the causes of defects involve matching the data on causes with corresponding data on their ef-

Equip-ment	Worker	Mon.		Tue.		Wed.		Thu.		Fri.		Sat.	
		AM	PM	AM	PM	AM	PM	AM	PM	AM	PM	AM	PM
Machine 1	A	∞ ⨯ ●	o ⨯	∞∞	o ⨯⨯	∞∞ ⨯⨯⨯ ●	∞∞∞ ⨯⨯⨯	∞∞∞ ⨯ ●●	o ⨯⨯	∞∞∞	∞	o	⨯⨯ ●
	B	o ⨯⨯ ●	∞∞ ⨯⨯⨯ ●	∞∞∞∞ ⨯⨯	∞∞ ⨯⨯	∞∞∞∞ ⨯⨯ ●	∞∞∞∞ ⨯ ●	∞∞∞ ⨯⨯ ●●	∞∞ ⨯ ●	∞ ⨯⨯	∞∞∞ ⨯	∞	∞∞∞ ⨯⨯ ●
Machine 2	C	∞ ⨯	o ⨯	∞ ●		∞∞∞ ⨯	∞∞∞∞ ⨯ ●	∞	o	∞ △ □	∞	o △ □	o □
	D	∞ ⨯	o ⨯	∞ △ ●	∞∞ △ ●	∞∞ ⨯ ●	∞∞∞ ●	∞ △	∞ △△ □	∞ ●●	o	∞ ⨯ □	o ⨯⨯

○: surface scratch ⨯: blowhole △: defective finishing
●: improper shape □: others

Figure 2.4   Defect Cause Check Sheet

fects, keeping them in a neatly corresponding order, and later analyzing them by stratifying by causes or drawing scatter diagrams. But if the case is a simple one, it is possible to gather corresponding data with a check sheet.

For example, Figure 2.4 is a check sheet for recording defect occurrence in bakelite knobs, with regard to machines, workers, days, and types of defect. We can see at a glance that worker *B* produces a lot of defects. On Wednesday, all workers produced many defects. A search for the causes revealed that worker *B* was not changing dies often enough, and on Wednesdays raw materials had a composition which was more likely to cause defects.

A check sheet using a cause-and-effect diagram can be made for the same purpose. That is to say, a cause-and-effect diagram which will be easily understood by workers may be prepared, and the space near each arrow is check-marked when a cause or condition of a defect becomes known. From this, it is possible to determine which causes should be given priority for action.

Besides the examples already described, there are many other kinds of check sheet which are being employed in factories. Check sheets are designed by first considering the aim of collecting the data, and then making various creative modifications so that data can be gathered and recorded easily and in ways most suited to the objective.

Exercise 2.1
In a lens polishing process, there are two workers, each operating two machines. The fraction defective of this process has gone up lately. The workers are asking for a change of machinery, saying that the machines currently being used are too old. The staff in charge of the process says that the workers should be more careful because they are making careless mistakes. What would you do in this situation?

Chapter 3
Pareto Analysis

3.1 What Are Pareto Diagrams?

Quality problems appear in the form of loss (defective items and their cost). It is extremely important to clarify the distribution pattern of the loss. Most of the loss will be due to a very few types of defect, and these defects can be attributed to a very small number of causes. Thus, if the causes of these *vital few* defects are identified, we can eliminate almost all the losses by concentrating on these particular causes, leaving aside the other *trivial many* defects for the time being. By using the Pareto diagram, we can solve this type of problem efficiently.

In 1897, the Italian economist V. Pareto presented a formula showing that the distribution of income is uneven. A similar theory was expressed diagrammatically by the U.S. economist M.C. Lorenz in 1907. Both of these scholars pointed out that by far the largest share of income or wealth is held by a very small number of people. Meanwhile, in the field of quality control, Dr. J. M. Juran applied Lorenz's diagram method as a formula in order to classify problems of quality into the vital few and the trivial many, and named this method *Pareto Analysis*. He pointed out that in many cases, most defects and the cost of these arise from a relatively small number of causes.

3.2 How to Make Pareto Diagrams

Step 1
Decide what problems are to be investigated and how to collect the data.
1) Decide what kind of problems you want to investigate.
   Example: Defective items, losses in monetary terms, accidents occurring.
2) Decide what data will be necessary and how to classify them.
   Example: By type of defect, location, process, machine, worker, method.
   Note: Summarize items appearing infrequently under the heading "others."
3) Determine the method of collecting the data and the period during which it is to be collected.
   Note: Use of an investigation form is recommended.
Step 2
Design a data tally sheet listing the items, with space to record their totals (Table 3.1).
Step 3
Fill out the tally sheet and calculate the totals.
Step 4
Make a Pareto diagram data sheet listing the items, their individual totals, cumulative totals, percentages of overall total, and cumulative percentages (Table 3.2).

Table 3.1　Data Tally Sheet

Type of Defect	Tally	Total
Crack	𝈐𝈐 𝈐𝈐	10
Scratch	𝈐𝈐 𝈐𝈐 𝈐𝈐 𝈐𝈐 .... 𝈐𝈐 //	42
Stain	𝈐𝈐 /	6
Strain	𝈐𝈐 𝈐𝈐 𝈐𝈐 𝈐𝈐 .... 𝈐𝈐 ////	104
Gap	////	4
Pinhole	𝈐𝈐 𝈐𝈐 𝈐𝈐 𝈐𝈐	20
Others	𝈐𝈐 𝈐𝈐 ////	14
Total		200

Table 3.2   Data Sheet for Pareto Diagram

Type of Defect	Number of Defects	Cumulative Total	Percentage of Overall Total	Cumulative Percentage
Strain	104	104	52	52
Scratch	42	146	21	73
Pinhole	20	166	10	83
Crack	10	176	5	88
Stain	6	182	3	91
Gap	4	186	2	93
Others	14	200	7	100
Total	200	—	100	—

Step 5
Arrange the items in the order of quantity, and fill out the data sheet.
Note: The item "others" should be placed in the last line, no matter how large it is. This is because it is composed of a group of items each of which is smaller than the smallest item listed individually.

Step 6
Draw two vertical axes and a horizontal axis.
1) Vertical axes
   a) Left-hand vertical axis
      Mark this axis with a scale from 0 to the overall total.
   b) Right-hand vertical axis
      Mark this axis with a scale from 0% to 100%.
2) Horizontal axis
   Divide this axis into the number of intervals to the number of items classified.

Step 7
Construct a bar diagram.

Step 8
Draw the cumulative curve (Pareto curve).
Mark the cumulative values (cumulative total or cumulative percentage), above the right-hand intervals of each item, and connect the points by a solid line.

Step 9
Write any necessary items on the diagram.
1) Items concerning the diagram

Title, significant quantities, units, name of drawer.
2) Items concerning the data
Period, subject and place of investigations, total number of data.

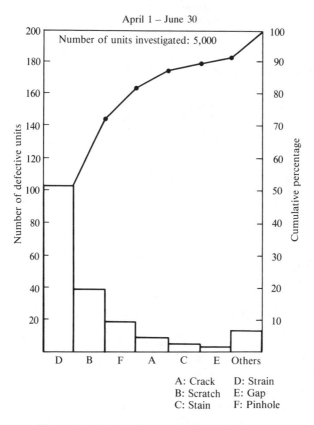

Figure 3.1   Pareto Diagram by Defective Items

3.3 Pareto Diagrams by Phenomena And Pareto Diagrams by Causes

As already mentioned, a Pareto diagram is a method of identifying the "vital few," and there are two types.

(1) Pareto Diagrams by Phenomena

This is a diagram concerning the following undesirable results, and is used to find out what the major problem is.

1) Quality: defects, faults, failures, complaints, returned items, repairs.
2) Cost: amount of loss, expenses.
3) Delivery: stock shortages, defaults in payments, delays in delivery.
4) Safety: accidents, mistakes, breakdowns.

(2) Pareto Diagrams by Causes

This is a diagram concerning causes in the process, and is used to find out what the major cause of the problem is.

1) Operator: shift, group, age, experience, skill, individual person.
2) Machine: machines, equipments, tools, organizations, models, instruments.
3) Raw material: manufacturer, plant, lot, kind.
4) Operation method: conditions, orders, arrangements, methods.

3.4 Notes on Pareto Diagrams

(1) Hints on Making Pareto Diagrams

1) Check various classifications and construct many kinds of Pareto diagrams.

   You can grasp the essence of a problem by observing it from various angles, and it is necessary to try out various methods of classification until you identify the vital few, which is the aim of Pareto analysis.

2) It is undesirable that "others" represent a higher percentage.

   If this happens, it is because the items for investigation are not classified appropriately and too many items fall under this heading. In this case, a different method of classification should be considered.

3) If a monetary value can be assigned to the data, it is best to draw the Pareto diagrams with the vertical axis showing this.

   If the financial implications of a problem are not properly appreciated, the research itself may end up as ineffective. Cost is an important scale of measurement in management.

(2) Hints on Using Pareto Diagrams

1) If an item is expected to be amenable to a simple solution, it should be tackled right away even if it is of relatively small importance.

   Since a Pareto diagram aims at efficient problem-solving, it basically requires us to tackle only the vital few. However, if an item which appears to be of relatively small importance is expected to be solved by a simple countermeasure, it will serve as an example of efficient problem-solving, and the experience, information and incentives to morale obtained through this will be of great assets for future problem-solving.

2) Do not fail to make a Pareto diagram by causes.

   After identifying the problem by making a Pareto diagram by phenomena, it is necessary to identify the causes in order to solve the problem. It is therefore vital to make a Pareto diagram by causes if any improvements are to be effected.

Exercise 3.1

Analyze the data in Table 3.3 by making various Pareto diagrams.

Table 3.3

Operator	Machine	Monday	Tuesday	Wednesday	Thursday	Friday
A	No. 1	•••• ** ○○ ## ☆	••••• * ○○○ #	••••• ***** ○○○○ ## ☆	•••• * ○○ ##	••••• * ○○○○ ## #
A	No. 2	•• * ○	••• ** ○○ ☆	••••• ***** ○○ #	•• * ○ #	•• ** ○ #
B	No. 3	••• ** ○ #	••• * ○	••••• ***** ○ #	••• * ○ # ☆	••• * ○○ #
B	No. 4	•• * ○○ ☆	••• * ○ #	••••• **** ○○ #	•• * #	•• * ○○ #

• Strain   * Scratch   ○ Pinhole   # Crack   ☆ Others

Chapter 4

Cause-and-Effect Diagrams

4.1 What Are Cause-and-Effect Diagrams?

The output or result of a process can be attributed to a multitude of factors, and a cause-and-effect relation can be found among those factors. We can determine the structure or a multiple cause-and-effect relation by observing it systematically. It is difficult to solve complicated problems without considering this structure, which consists of a chain of causes and effects, and a cause-and-effect diagram is a method of expressing it simply and easily.

In 1953, Kaoru Ishikawa, Professor of the University of Tokyo, summarized the opinions of engineers at a plant in the form of a cause-and-effect diagram as they discussed a quality problem. This is said to be the first time this approach was used. Prior to this, the staff of Professor Ishikawa's had been using the method for arranging factors in their research activities. When the diagram was used practically, it proved to be very useful and soon came to be widely used among companies throughout Japan. It was included in the JIS (Japanese Industrial Standards) terminology of Quality Control, and was defined as follows:
Cause-and-effect diagram:
   a diagram which shows the relation between a quality characteristic and factors.

The diagram is now used not only for treating the quality characteristics of products, but also in other fields, and has found application worldwide.

4.2 How to Make Cause-and-Effect Diagrams

Making a useful cause-and-effect diagram is no easy task. It may safely be said that those who succeed in problem-solving in quality control are those who succeed in making a useful cause-and-effect diagram. There are many ways of making the diagram, but two typical methods will be described here. Prior to introducing the procedures, the structure of the cause-and-effect diagram is explained with an example.

(1) Structure of Cause-and-Effect Diagrams and Example

A cause-and-effect diagram is also called a "fishbone diagram" since it looks like the skeleton of a fish, as shown in the Figure 4.1. It is also occasionally called a "tree" or "river" diagram, but the name "fishbone" is used here. An actual example is shown as Figure 4.2.

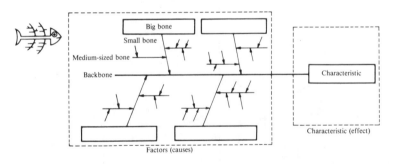

Figure 4.1 Structure of Cause-and-Effect Diagram

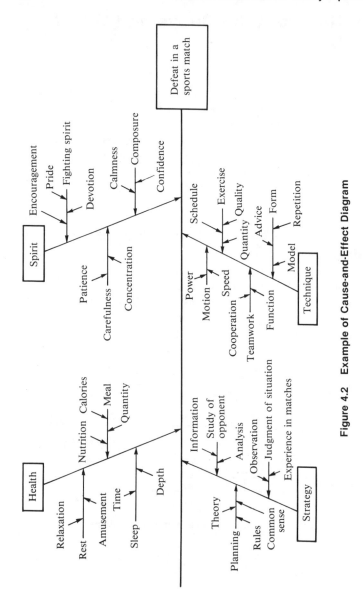

Figure 4.2　Example of Cause-and-Effect Diagram

(2) Procedure for Making Cause-and-Effect Diagrams For Identifying Causes

1) Procedure
Step 1
Determine the quality characteristic.
Step 2
Choose one quality characteristic and write it on the right-hand side of a sheet of paper, draw in the backbone from left to right, and enclose the characteristic in a square. Next, write the primary causes which affect the quality characteristic as big bones also enclosed by squares.
Step 3
Write the causes (secondary causes) which affect the big bones (primary causes) as medium-sized bones, and write the causes (tertiary causes) which affect the medium-sized bones as small bones.
Step 4
Assign an importance to each factor, and mark the particularly important factors that seem to have a significant effect on the quality characteristic.
Step 5
Record any necessary information.

2) Explanation of the procedure
You may often find it difficult to proceed when you practice this approach. The best method in such a case is to consider the "variation." For example, consider variation in the quality characteristic when you are thinking about the big bones. If the data shows that such a variation exists, consider why it exists. A variation in the effect must be caused by variation in the factors. This kind of switchover of thought is extremely effective.

When you are making a cause-and-effect diagram relating to a certain defect, for example, you may discover that there is a variation in the number of defects occuring on different days of a week. If you find that the defect occurred more frequently on Monday than on any other day of the week, you can change your thinking as follows: "Why did the defect occur?" "Why did the defect occur more frequently on Monday than on any other day of the week?" This will lead you to look for factors which make Monday and other days different, eventually leading you to discover the cause of the defect.

By adopting this method of thinking at each stage of examining the relation between the characteristic and the big bones, the big bones and the medium-sized bones, and the medium-sized bones and the small bones, it is possible to construct a useful cause-and-effect diagram on a logical basis.

Having completed the cause-and-effect diagram, the next step is to assign an importance to each factor. All the factors in the diagram are not necessarily closely related to the characteristic. Mark those factors which seem to have a particularly significant effect on the characteristics.

Finally, include any necessary information in the diagram, such as the title, the name of the product, process or group, a list of participants, the date, etc.

(3) Procedure for Making Cause-and-Effect Diagrams For Systematically Listing Causes

1) Procedure
Step 1
Decide on the quality characteristic.
Step 2
Find as many causes as possible which are considered to affect the quality characteristic.
Step 3
Sort out the relations among the causes and make a cause-and-effect diagram by connecting those elements with the quality characteristic by cause-and-effect relations.
Step 4
Assign an importance to each factor, and mark the particularly important factors which seem to have a significant effect on the quality characteristic.
Step 5
Write in any necessary information.

2) Explanation of the procedure
This approach is characterized by linking two different activities: picking up as many causes as possible and arranging them systematically.

For picking up causes, open and active discussion is required, and an effective method of conducting a meeting held for this purpose is brain-storming, invented by A.F. Osborn in the United States.

In making the cause-and-effect diagram, the causes should be arranged systematically by proceeding from the small bones to the medium-sized bones, and then from the medium-sized bones to the big bones.

4.3 Notes on Cause-and-Effect Diagrams

(1) Hints on Making Cause-and-Effect Diagrams

1) Identify all the relevant factors through examination and discussion by many people.
   The factors most strongly influencing the characteristic must be determined from among those listed in the diagram. If a factor is left out in the initial discussion stage before the diagram is constructed, it will not appear at a later stage. Consequently, discussion by all the persons concerned is indispensable to the preparation of a complete diagram which has no omissions.
2) Express the characteristic as concretely as possible.
   Characteristic expressed in an abstract term will only result in a cause-and-effect diagram based on generalities. Although such a diagram will contain no basic mistakes from the point of view of cause-and-effect relations, it will not be very useful for solving actual problems.
3) Make the same number of cause-and-effect diagrams as that of characteristics.
   Errors in the weight and the length of the same product will have different cause-and-effect structures, and these should be analyzed in two separate diagrams. Trying to include everything in one diagram will result in a diagram which is unmanageably large and complicated, making problem-solving very difficult.
4) Choose a measurable characteristic and factors.
   After completing a cause-and-effect diagram, it is necessary to grasp the strength of the cause-and-effect relation objectively using data. For this purpose, both the characteristic and the

causal factors should be measurable. When it is impossible to measure them, you should try to make them measurable, or find substitute characteristics.

5) Discover factors amenable to action.

If the cause you have identified cannot be acted upon, the problem will not be solved. If improvements are to be effected, the causes should be broken down to the level at which they can be acted upon, otherwise identifying them will become a meaningless exercise.

(2) Hints on Using Cause-and-Effect Diagrams

1) Assign an importance to each factor objectively on the basis of data.

Examination of factors on the basis of your own skill and experience is important, but it is dangerous to give importance to them through subjective perceptions or impressions alone. Most of the problems which can be solved by such an approach might have already been solved, and consequently, most of the problems remaining unsolved cannot be solved by this approach. Assigning importance to factors objectively using data is both more scientific and more logical.

2) Try to improve the cause-and-effect diagram continually while using it.

Actually using a cause-and-effect diagram will help you see those parts which need to be checked, deleted or modified, and also to discover parts which should be added. You should make repeated efforts to improve your diagram, and eventually a really useful diagram will be obtained. This will be useful in solving problems, and at the same time, will help improve your own skill and to increase your technological knowledge.

4.4 Pareto Diagrams and Cause-and-Effect Diagrams

Various methods should be applied in combination in solving problems, and the combination of a Pareto diagram and a cause-and-effect diagram is particularly useful. The following is a typical example of this.

(1) Selection of Problems

Here is an example illustrating the examination of non-conformity in a manufacturing process by the use of a Pareto diagram. When data on non-conformity collected over two months was classified by non-conforming items, it was found that dimensional defectives were largest in number, constituting 48 percent of the total non-conformance. We therefore tried to reduce the number of non-conformity with stress on dimensional defectives.

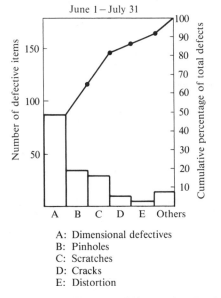

A: Dimensional defectives
B: Pinholes
C: Scratches
D: Cracks
E: Distortion

Figure 4.3   Pareto Diagram of Non-conforming Items

(2) Analysis and Countermeasures

All the shop members discussed the causes of the dimensional variation and constructed a cause-and-effect diagram (See Figure 4.4). A Pareto diagram by causes (Figure 4.5) was then made by investigating all the units with dimensional variation in order to examine to what extent these factors were affecting the non-conformance. With some items, it was impossible to clarify the causes of the non-conformance, and these were lumped together under the heading "Unclear." We discovered from the Pareto diagram that the occurrence of the defect was greatly affected by the fitting position. Although the fitting position had been stipulated by the traditional operational standard, the standard fitting method was not shown. This led to variation in the fitting position, and resulted in the dimensional defectives. The shop members therefore designed a suitable fitting method, which was further standardized and added to the operational standards.

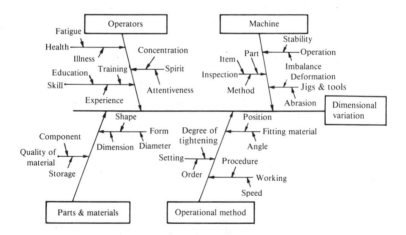

Figure 4.4   Cause-and-Effect Diagram of Dimensional Defectives

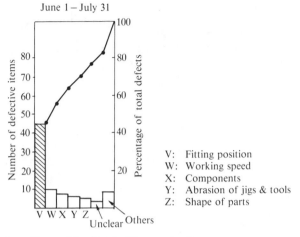

Figure 4.5 Pareto Diagram by Causes

(3) Effects of Improvement

After the improvement was carried out, data was collected, and a Pareto diagram was made to compare the results. The following two Pareto diagrams clearly show that dimensional defectives were reduced.

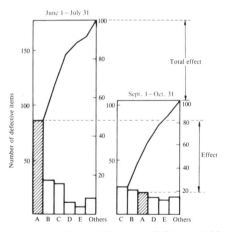

Figure 4.6 Comparison of Pareto Diagrams Before and After Improvement

Exercise 4.1

Make a cause-and-effect diagram as to the following characteristics:
1) Typing errors (mistyping).
2) Dialling the wrong telephone number.
3) Being late for an appointment.

Chapter **5**

Histograms

5.1 Distributions and Histograms

(1) Variation and Distribution

If we could collect data from a process in which all factors (man, machine, material, method, etc.) were perfectly constant, all the data would have the same values. In reality, however, it is impossible to keep all factors in a constant state all the time. Strictly speaking, even some factors which, we assume, are in a constant state cannot be perfectly constant. It is inevitable for the values in a given set of data to have a variation. The values of the data are not the same all the time, but this does not mean that they are determined in a disorderly fashion. Although the values change every time, they are governed by a certain rule, and this situation is referred to as data following a certain distribution.

(2) Populations and Samples

In quality control, we try to discover facts by collecting data and then take necessary action based on those facts. The data is not collected as an end in itself, but as a means of finding out the facts behind the data.

For example, consider a sampling inspection. We take a sample from a lot, carry out measurements on it, and then decide whether we should accept the whole lot or not. Here our concern is not the sample itself, but the quality of the whole lot. As another example, consider the control of a manufacturing process using an $\bar{x}$-R control chart. Our purpose is not to determine the characteristics of the sample taken for drawing the $\bar{x}$-R chart, but to find out what state the process is in.

The totality of items under consideration is called the *population*.

In the first example above, the population is the lot, and in the second it is the process.

Some people may feel it difficult to regard a "process" as a "population" because while a "lot" is indeed a group of finite individual objects, a "process" itself is not a product at all, but is made up of the 5M's (man, machine, material, method, and measurement). When we turn our attention to product-making function, we will recognize that the "process" produces unmistakably a group of products. Moreover, the number of products is infinite unless the "process" stops producing them, and for this reason, a process is considered to be an infinite population.

One or more items taken from a population intended to provide information on the population is called a *sample*. Since a sample is used for estimating the characteristics of the entire population, it should be chosen in such a way as to reflect the characteristics of the population. A commonly-used sampling method is to choose any member of the population with equal probability. This method is called *random sampling,* and a sample taken by random sampling is called a *random sample.*

We obtain data by measuring the characteristics of a sample. Using this data, we draw an inference about the population, and then take some remedial action. However, the measured value of a

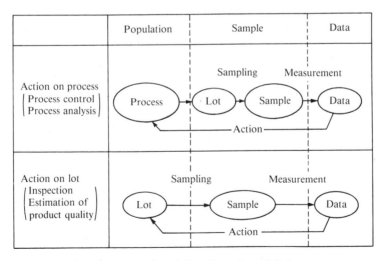

Figure 3.1 **Population, Sample and Data**

sample will vary according to the sample taken, making it difficult to decide what action is necessary. Statistical analysis will tell us how to interpret such data. The details will be explained in Chapter 9. Figure 5.1 shows the relation between population, sample, and data.

(3) Histograms

The data obtained from a sample serves as a basis for a decision on the population. The larger the sample size is, the more information we get about the population. But an increase of sample size also means an increase in the amount of data, and it becomes difficult to understand the population from these data even when they are arranged into tables. In such a case, we need a method which will enable us to understand the population at a glance. A histogram answers our needs. By organizing many data into a histogram, we can understand the population in an objective manner.

5.2 How to Make Histograms

(1) How to Make Frequency Tables

Example 5.1
To investigate the distribution of the diameters of steel shafts produced in a grinding process, the diameters of 90 shafts are measured as shown in Table 5.1. Let us make a histogram using these data.

Table 5.1 Raw Data

Sample Number	Results of Measurement									
1 – 10	2.510	2.517	2.522	2.522	2.510	2.511	2.519	2.532	2.543	2.525
11 – 20	2.527	2.536	2.506	2.541	2.512	2.515	2.521	2.536	2.529	2.524
21 – 30	2.529	2.523	2.523	2.523	2.519	2.528	2.543	2.538	2.518	2.534
31 – 40	2.520	2.514	2.512	2.534	2.526	2.530	2.532	2.526	2.523	2.520
41 – 50	2.535	2.523	2.526	2.525	2.532	2.522	2.502	2.530	2.522	2.514
51 – 60	2.533	2.510	2.542	2.524	2.530	2.521	2.522	2.535	2.540	2.528
61 – 70	2.525	2.515	2.520	2.519	2.526	2.527	2.522	2.542	2.540	2.528
71 – 80	2.531	2.545	2.524	2.522	2.520	2.519	2.519	2.529	2.522	2.513
81 – 90	2.518	2.527	2.511	2.519	2.531	2.527	2.529	2.528	2.519	2.521

Procedure

Step 1 Calculate the range (R)

Obtain the largest and the smallest of observed values and calculate R.

R = (the largest observed value) − (the smallest observed value)

The largest and the smallest of observed values can be easily obtained in the following manner:

Obtain the maximum and the minimum of values from each line of the table of observations, then take the largest of the maximum values and the smallest of the minimum values. These will be the maximum and the minimum of all of the observed values.

Example

Step 1 Calculate R

R is obtained from the largest and the smallest of observed values. (See Table 5.2.)

The largest value = 2.545
The smallest value = 2.502

Therefore,

$$R = 2.545 - 2.502 = 0.043.$$

Table 5.2   Table for Range Calculation

Sample Number	Results of Measurement										Maximum Value of the Line	Minimum Value of the Line
1 − 10	2.510	2.517	2.522	2.522	2.510	2.511	2.519	2.532	2.543	2.525	2.543	2.510
11 − 20	2.527	2.536	2.506	2.541	2.512	2.515	2.521	2.536	2.529	2.524	2.541	2.506
21 − 30	2.529	2.523	2.523	2.523	2.519	2.528	2.543	2.538	2.518	2.534	2.543	2.518
31 − 40	2.520	2.514	2.512	2.534	2.526	2.530	2.532	2.526	2.523	2.520	2.534	2.512

41–50	2.535	2.523	2.526	2.525	2.532	2.522	2.502	2.530	2.522	2.514	2.535	2.502
51–60	2.533	2.510	2.542	2.524	2.530	2.521	2.522	2.535	2.540	2.528	2.542	2.510
61–70	2.525	2.515	2.520	2.519	2.526	2.527	2.522	2.542	2.540	2.528	2.542	2.515
71–80	2.531	2.545	2.524	2.522	2.520	2.519	2.519	2.529	2.522	2.513	2.545	2.513
81–90	2.518	2.527	2.511	2.519	2.531	2.527	2.529	2.528	2.519	2.521	2.531	2.511
											The Largest Value 2.545	The Smallest Value 2.502

Step 2 Determine the class interval

The class interval is determined so that the range, which includes the maximum and the minimum of values, is divided into intervals of equal breadth. To obtain the interval breadth, divide R by 1, 2 or 5 (or 10, 20, 50; 0.1, 0.2, 0.5, etc.) so as to obtain from 5 to 20 class intervals of equal breadth. When there are two possibilities, use the narrower interval if the number of measured values is 100 or over and the wider interval, if there are 99 or less observed values.

Step 3 Prepare the frequency table form

Prepare a form, as in Table 5.3, on which the class, mid-point, frequency marks, frequency, etc., can be recorded.

Step 2 Determine the class interval

$0.043 \div 0.002 = 21.5$, and we make this 22 by rounding up to the nearest integer.

$0.043 \div 0.005 = 8.6$, and we make this 9 by rounding up to the nearest integer.

$0.043 \div 0.010 = 4.3$, and we make this 4 by rounding down to the nearest integer.

Thus, the class interval is determined as 0.005, since this gives a number of intervals between 5 and 20.

Step 3 Prepare the frequency table

Prepare a table as shown in Table 5.3.

Step 4 Determine the class boundaries

Determine the boundaries of the intervals so that they include the smallest and the largest of values, and write these down on the frequency table.

First, determine the lower boundary of the first class and add the interval breadth to this to obtain the boundary between the first and second classes. When you do so, make sure that the first class contains the smallest value and that the boundary value falls on 1/2 of the unit of measurement. Then keep adding the breadth of the interval to the previous value to obtain the second boundary, the third, and so on, and make sure that the last class includes the maximum value.

Step 5 Calculate the mid-point of class

Using the following equation, calculate the mid-point of class, and write this down on the frequency table.
Mid-point of the first class

$$= \frac{\text{Sum of the upper and lower boundaries of the first class}}{2},$$

Step 4 Determine the class boundaries

The boundaries of the first class should be determined as 2.5005 and 2.5055 so that the class includes the smallest value 2.502; the boundaries of the second class should be determined as $2.5055 - 2.5105$, and so on. Record these on a frequency Table. (See Table 5.3.)

Step 5 Calculate the mid-point of class

Mid-point of the first class

$$= \frac{2.5005 + 2.5055}{2} = 2.503,$$

Mid-point of the second class

$$= \frac{\text{Sum of the upper and lower boundaries of the second class}}{2},$$

and so on.

The mid-points of the second class, the third class, and so on, may also be obtained as follows:

Mid-point of the second class
= mid-point of the first class + class interval,

Mid-point of the third class
= mid-point of the second class + class interval,

and so on.

Step 6 *Obtain the frequencies*

Read the observed values one by one and record the frequencies falling in each class using tally marks, in groups of five, as follows:

Frequency	1	2	3	4	5
Frequency notation	/	//	///	////	卌

Frequency	6	7	...	...
Frequency notation	卌 /	卌 //	...	

Mid-point of the second class

$$\frac{2.5055 + 2.5105}{2} = 2.508,$$

and so on.

Step 6 *Obtain the frequencies*

Record the frequencies. (See Table 5.3.)

Table 5.3　Frequency Table

	Class	Mid-Point of Class x	Frequency Marks (Tally)	Frequency f
1	2.5005 − 2.5055	2.503	/	1
2	2.5055 − 2.5105	2.508	////	4
3	2.5105 − 2.5155	2.513	卌 ////	9
4	2.5155 − 2.5205	2.518	卌 卌 ////	14
5	2.5205 − 2.5255	2.523	卌 卌 卌 卌 //	22
6	2.5255 − 2.5305	2.528	卌 卌 卌 ////	19
7	2.5305 − 2.5355	2.533	卌 卌	10
8	2.5355 − 2.5405	2.538	卌	5
9	2.5405 − 2.5455	2.543	卌 /	6
	Total		—	90

Notes: 1. There would be an error in frequency marking (tallying) if the sum of the frequency f, (Σf), did not equal the total number (n) of observed values.
2. If the relative frequency is required, it can be obtained by dividing the frequency f by n.

(2) How to Make Histograms

Procedure	Example *(Example 5.1)*
Step 1 On a sheet of squared paper, mark the horizontal axis with a scale. The scale should not be on the base of class interval but it is better to be on the base of unit of measurement of data, 10 grams correspond to 10 mm, for example. This makes it convenient to make comparisons with many histograms which describe similar factors and characteristics as well as with specifications (standards). Leave a space about equal to the class interval on the horizontal axis on each side of the first and the last classes. *Step 2* Mark the left-hand vertical axis with a frequency scale, and, if necessary, draw the right-hand axis and mark it with a relative frequency scale. The height of the class with the maximum frequency should be from 0.5 to 2.0 times the distance between the maximum and the minimum values on the horizontal axis.	

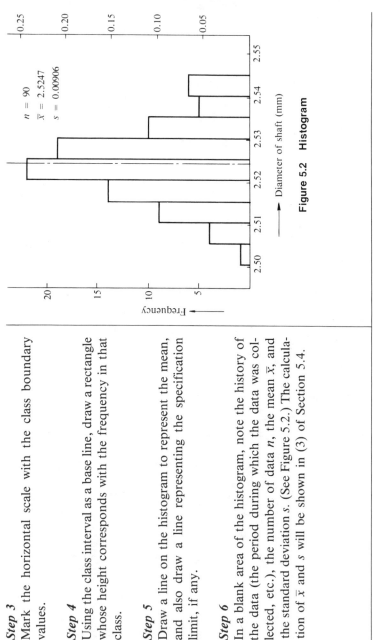

Figure 5.2   Histogram

Step 3
Mark the horizontal scale with the class boundary values.

Step 4
Using the class interval as a base line, draw a rectangle whose height corresponds with the frequency in that class.

Step 5
Draw a line on the histogram to represent the mean, and also draw a line representing the specification limit, if any.

Step 6
In a blank area of the histogram, note the history of the data (the period during which the data was collected, etc.), the number of data n, the mean $\bar{x}$, and the standard deviation s. (See Figure 5.2.) The calculation of $\bar{x}$ and s will be shown in (3) of Section 5.4.

5.3 How to Read Histograms

(1) Types of Histogram

It is possible to obtain useful information about the state of a population by looking at the shape of the histogram. The followings are typical shapes, and we can use them as clues for analyzing a process. (See Figure 5.3.)

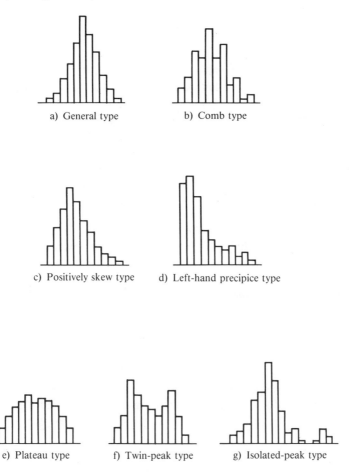

a) General type   b) Comb type

c) Positively skew type   d) Left-hand precipice type

e) Plateau type   f) Twin-peak type   g) Isolated-peak type

Figure 5.3   Types of Histogram

a) **General type** (symmetrical or bell-shaped)
Shape:
The mean value of the historgram is in the middle of the range of data. The frequency is the highest in the middle and becomes gradually lower towards the ends. The shape is symmetrical.
Note:
This is the shape which occurs most often.

b) **Comb type** (multi-modal type)
Shape:
Every other class has a lower frequency.
Note:
This shape occurs when the number of units of data included in the class varies from class to class or when there is a particular tendency in the way data is rounded off.

c) **Positively skew type** (Negatively skew type)
Shape:
The mean value of the histogram is located to the left (right) of the center of range. The frequency decreases somewhat abruptly towards the left (right), but gently towards the right (left). Asymmetrical.
Note:
This shape occurs when the lower (upper) limit is controlled either theoretically or by a specification value or when values lower (upper) than a certain value do not occur.

d) **Left-hand precipice type** (Right-hand precipice type)
Shape:
The mean value of the histogram is located far to the left (right) of the center of range. The frequency decreases abruptly on the left (right), and gently towards the right (left). Asymmetrical.
Note:
This is a shape which frequently occurs when a 100% screening has been done because of low process capability, and also when positive (negative) skewness becomes even more extreme.

e) **Plateau type**
Shape:
The frequency in each class forms a plateau because the classes

have more or less the same frequency except for those at the ends.
Note:
This shape occurs with a mixture of several distributions having different mean values.

f) Twin-peak type (bimodal type)
Shape:
The frequency is low near the middle of the range of data, and there is a peak on either side.
Note:
This shape occurs when two distributions with widely different mean values are mixed.

g) Isolated-peak type
Shape:
There is a small isolated peak in addition to a general-type histogram.
Note:
This is a shape which appears when there is a small inclusion of data from a different distribution, such as in the case of process abnormality, measurement error, or inclusion of data from a different process.

(2) Comparing Histograms With Specification Limits

If there is a specification, draw lines of the specification limits on the histogram to compare the distribution with the specification. Then see if the histogram is located well within the limits. Five typical cases as in the Figure 5.4 are described below. Use these as a reference for evaluating the population.

When the histogram satisfies the specification,
a) Maintenance of the present state is all that is needed, since the histogram amply satisfies the specification.
b) The specification is satisfied, but there is no extra margin. Therefore, it is better to reduce the variation by a small degree.

When the histogram does not satisfy the specification,

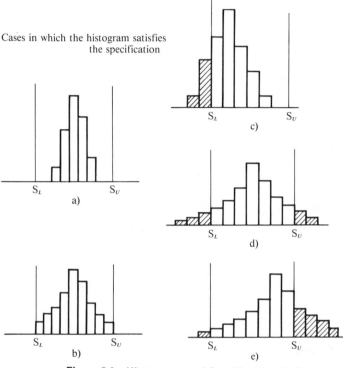

Figure 5.6　Histograms and Specification Limits

c) It is necessary to take measures to bring the mean closer to the middle of the specification.

d) This requires action to reduce the variation.

e) The measures described in both c) and d) are required.

(3) Stratification of Histograms

When the observed values are divided into two or more sub-populations according to the condition which existed at the time of data collection, such subpopulations are called *strata*, and dividing data into strata is called *stratification*.

The observed values are always accompanied by some variation. Therefore, when the data is stratified according to the factors which are thought to cause variation, the causes of variation become more easily detectable. This method can be used effectively to raise product quality by reducing variation and improving the process average.

Stratification is usually done according to materials, machines, conditions of operation, and workers.

5.4 Measures to Represent the Characteristics of Distributions

(1) Means and Standard Deviations

The value of the measured characteristic of a sample taken from a population will vary, and cannot be known until it is observed. Such a variable is called a *random variable*. The quality characteristics of factory-made products have such a nature.

When handling such data, it is often more convenient to regard each item of data as a whole set rather than treating each of them individually. In order to see the data as a group, first we determine the center of the data, and then study how each data item is concentrated around the center.

A typical measure for expressing the center is *mean* or *expectation*. When we have obtained n data items, $x_1, \ldots, x_n$, the mean of this data is given by

$$\bar{x} = \frac{1}{n} \sum_{i=1}^{n} x_i, \tag{5.1}$$

but for the set as a whole, the mean is given by

$$\mu = \Sigma \, xP(x), \tag{5.2}$$

or

$$\mu = \int xf(x)\,dx, \tag{5.3}$$

where $P(x)$ is the probability and $f(x)$ is the probability density of the random variable x.

$\bar{x}$ is the mean of the data obtained, and is called the *sample mean*. μ is the mean of the whole set with which we are concerned and called the *population mean*.

Variance and *standard deviation* are among the measures used to express the degree of concentration of data around the center. When we have obtained n data items, x_1, ..., x_n, the variance of this data is expressed by

$$V = \frac{1}{n-1} \sum_{i=1}^{n} (x_i - \bar{x})^2,$$ (5.4)

and the standard deviation is expressed by

$$s = \sqrt{V}.$$ (5.5)

The variance of a population is given by

$$\sigma^2 = \Sigma (x - \mu)^2 P(x),$$ (5.6)

or

$$\sigma^2 = \int (x - \mu)^2 f(x)\, dx$$ (5.7)

and the standard deviation, which is the square root of variance , is expressed as σ.

Variance is the mean of the square of the difference between the individual data item and the mean. Large vairance means large variation in the data.

V and s are values pertaining to the data, and are called *sample variance* and *sample standard deviation*, respectively. σ^2 and σ are values concerning a population and are called *population variance* and *population standard deviation,* respectively.

(2) Calculation of Means and Standard Deviations

Example 5.2
The followings are the measurements of dimension of some machine part. Calculate the mean and the standard deviation.

13.42   13.62   13.56   13.66   13.48   13.52   13.57

In some cases, data transformation

$$X_i = (x_i - a) \times h \tag{5.8}$$

may be done to facilitate the calculation. Then

$$\bar{x} = a + \frac{1}{h}\,\bar{X}, \tag{5.9}$$

$$S = \sum_{i=1}^{n} (x_i - \bar{x})^2 = \frac{1}{h^2} \sum_{i=1}^{n} (X_i - \bar{X})^2$$

$$= \frac{1}{h^2} \left\{ \Sigma X_i^2 - \frac{1}{n}(\Sigma X_i)^2 \right\}, \tag{5.10}$$

$$V = S / (n - 1), \tag{5.11}$$

$$s = \sqrt{V}. \tag{5.12}$$

In this example, let a and h be 13.40 and 100, respectively. Then we obtain the following table (Table 5.4).

Table 5.4

x	X	X^2
13.42	2	4
13.62	22	484
13.56	16	256
13.66	26	676
13.48	8	64
13.52	12	144
13.57	17	289
Total	103	1917

$$\bar{X} = \frac{103}{7} = 14.7$$

From (5.9)

$$\bar{x} = 13.40 + \frac{1}{100} \times 14.7 = 13.547$$

From (5.10)

$$S = \frac{1}{100^2} \left\{ 1917 - \frac{1}{7} \times 103^2 \right\} = 4.01 \times 10^{-2}$$

$$V = 4.01 \times 10^{-2}/(7-1) = 0.669 \times 10^{-2}$$

$$s = \sqrt{0.669 \times 10^{-2}} = 0.082$$

(3) Calculation of Means and Standard Deviations From Frequency Tables

Let us calculate the mean and the standard deviation of the diameters of 90 shafts as shown in Table 5.1. When the number of data is large and the data is summarized in a frequency table, the mean and the standard deviation are calculated as follows:

Procedure	Example *(Example 5.1)*
Step 1 Prepare a calculation form as in Table 5.5.	
Step 2 Write down the class boundaries, the mid-points of classes, and frequency f.	

Table 5.5   Calculation Table

No.	Class	Mid-point x	Frequency f	u	uf	u^2f
1	2.5005 — 2.5055	2.503	1	−4	−4	16
2	2.5055 — 2.5105	2.508	4	−3	−12	36
3	2.5105 — 2.5155	2.513	9	−2	−18	36
4	2.5155 — 2.5205	2.518	14	−1	−14	14
5	2.5205 — 2.5255	2.523	22	0	0	0
6	2.5255 — 2.5305	2.528	19	1	19	19
7	2.5305 — 2.5355	2.533	10	2	20	40
8	2.5355 — 2.5405	2.538	5	3	15	45
9	2.5405 — 2.5455	2.543	6	4	24	96
	Total		90	—	30	302

Step 3

Assign the mid-point 0 ($u = 0$) to the class which has the maximum f, and write 0 in the u column. Write -1, -2, … towards the smaller observed values, and 1, 2, … towards the larger measured values.

The relationship between x and u is expressed by the following equation:

$$u = (x-a)/h, \tag{5.13}$$

where,

　a: the mid-point of the class where $u = 0$,
　h: the class interval.

Step 4

Enter the products of u and f in the uf column, and the products of u and uf in the u^2f column; obtain the sum of each, and record these in the relevant spaces.

$$\Sigma uf = u_1 f_1 + u_2 f_2 + \cdots$$
$$\Sigma u^2 f = u_1^2 f_1 + u_2^2 f_2 + \cdots$$

Step 3

Assign 0 to the mid-point of u of class no. 5.

　$a = 2.523$
　$h = 0.005$

Step 4

No. 1　$uf = (-4) \times 1 = -4$

No. 2　$uf = (-3) \times 4 = -12$

$\qquad \vdots$

No. 1　$u^2 f = uf \times u = (-4) \times (-4) = 16$

No. 2　$u^2 f = uf \times u = (-12) \times (-3) = 36$

$\qquad \vdots$

$$\Sigma uf = (-4) + (-12) + \cdots + 24 = 30$$
$$\Sigma u^2 f = 16 + 36 + \cdots + 96 = 302$$

Step 5

Calculate $\bar{x}$ using the following equation:

$$\bar{x} = a + h \ (\Sigma uf/n).$$ (5.14)

Step 5

$$\bar{x} = 2.523 + 0.005 \times \frac{30}{90}$$
$$= 2.523 + 0.00167$$
$$= 2.52467 \ (\text{mm})$$

Step 6

Calculate s using the following equation:

$$s = h\sqrt{(\Sigma u^2 f - \frac{(\Sigma uf)^2}{n}) / (n-1)}.$$ (5.15)

Step 6

$$s = 0.005 \times \sqrt{(302 - \frac{30^2}{90}) / (90-1)}$$
$$= 0.005 \times \sqrt{3.2809}$$
$$= 0.00906 \ (\text{mm})$$

5.5 Normal Distribution and Its Characteristics

(1) Normal Distribution

A histogram is constructed from a certain number of data. But what would happen to the histogram if we kept on increasing the number of data? If the class interval is reduced little by little while the number of data is increased, a smooth frequency distribution curve is obtained as the limit of a relative frequency distribution. It is indeed an expression of the population itself, since it is obtained from an infinite number of data.

There are many kinds of distributions, and the most typical one is the *normal distribution*. When the variation of a quality characteristic is caused by the sum of a large number of independent infinitesimal errors due to different factors, the distribution of the quality characteristic becomes in many cases approximately a normal distribution. Normal distribution can be simply described as having the shape of a bell or mountain, and in a more detailed description,

a) the frequency is the highest in the middle and becomes gradually lower towards the tails, and

b) it is symmetrical.

This curve can be expressed mathematically as follows:

$$f(x) = \frac{1}{\sqrt{2\pi}\sigma} e^{-\frac{(x-\mu)^2}{2\sigma^2}} . \tag{5.16}$$

Figure 5.5 shows the shape of this distribution.

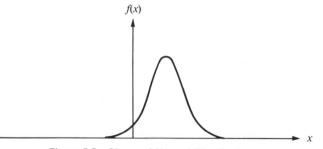

Figure 5.5   Shape of Normal Distribution

(2) Characteristics of Normal Distribution

As we can see from equation (5.16), the equation of the normal distribution has the two parameters, μ and σ^2.

Normal distribution is uniquely determined by these two parameters and denoted simply by $N(\mu, \sigma^2)$. These two parameters have the following meanings.

μ: the center of the distribution (the mean)

σ: the spread of the distribution (the standard deviation)

They can be described graphically as in Figure 5.6.

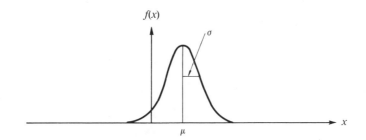

Figure 5.6 Normal Distribution and Its Parameters

To obtain a probability in a normal distribution, we standardize and use the normal distribution table. *Standardization* is to transform a variable x to

$$u = \frac{x - \mu}{\sigma}. \tag{5.17}$$

We then have the standard measure u, which is distributed as the *standard normal distribution* $N(0, 1^2)$. The *normal distribution table* gives probabilities in the standard normal distribution. (See Table A. 1 of the Appendix.)

Let us consider the probability that a random variable x from $N(\mu, \sigma^2)$ falls inside the limits $\mu \pm u\sigma$. Figure 5.7 shows the probability for various values of u. Theoretically, a normal variate can take any value between $-\infty$ and $+\infty$. But, from the figure we have 99.7% for $u = 3$. This means that in practice we can neglect the chance that x will fall outside the limits $\mu \pm 3\sigma$. This fact is an important rule of the normal distribution, and is called the 3-*sigma rule*. It is the basis for determining the control limits in a control chart.

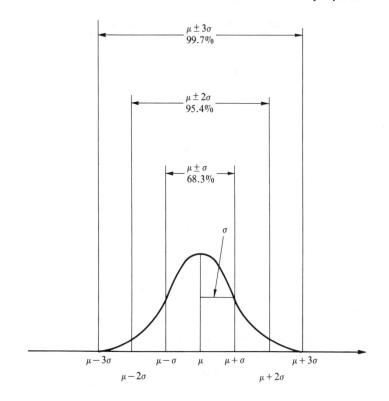

Figure 5.7 μ, σ and Probability of Normal Distribution

(3) Process Capability Index

After histogram shows that it follows normal distribution, a study of process capabilities is often undertaken. This is to find out whether the process can meet specifications or not. If we assume the process is normally distributed, we can immediately determine the percent defective from the given specifications and parameters (μ, σ). But it is more useful to evaluate the process by using C_P (Process Capability Index). The definition of C_P is as follows:

Both-sided specifications $(S_U$ and $S_L)$

$$C_P = \frac{S_U - S_L}{6s}. \qquad (5.18)$$

One-sided specification $(S_U$ or $S_L)$

$$C_P = \frac{S_U - \bar{x}}{3s} \qquad (5.19)$$

or

$$C_P = \frac{\bar{x} - S_L}{3s}. \qquad (5.20)$$

And the evaluation of process by using C_P is as follows:
1) $1.33 \leqq C_P$ satisfiable enough
2) $1.00 \leqq C_P < 1.33$ adequate
3) $C_P < 1.00$ inadequate

Example 5.3
Table 5.6 shows the yields from a certain chemical reaction process. Since two reaction vessels, *A* and *B*, were used for this reaction, it was pointed out that perhaps there was a difference between them. Stratification was carried out according to the reaction vessels, and the results are shown in Figure 5.8. Differences were found between two reaction vessels.

Table 5.6 Stratification of Data

No.	R.V.	x	No.	R.V.	x	No.	R.V.	x	No.	R.V.	x
1	A	84.9	26	B	86.2	51	B	86.6	76	B	85.4
2	A	83.8	27	B	87.2	52	B	87.0	77	B	84.6
3	B	86.2	28	A	83.0	53	B	86.7	78	A	83.9
4	B	85.7	29	B	86.3	54	A	84.9	79	A	83.2
5	A	83.9	30	A	83.9	55	A	83.7	80	B	85.7
6	B	86.4	31	A	83.5	56	B	84.7	81	B	86.9
7	B	86.8	32	B	84.1	57	A	85.1	82	A	84.0
8	B	87.0	33	B	84.7	58	B	85.4	83	B	85.7
9	A	83.8	34	A	85.3	59	A	84.4	84	A	84.3
10	B	86.0	35	A	84.5	60	A	84.2	85	B	86.0
11	B	86.3	36	A	84.5	61	B	85.8	86	A	83.6
12	A	83.0	37	B	86.2	62	A	85.1	87	B	86.0
13	A	83.5	38	A	84.1	63	A	84.4	88	A	83.6
14	A	82.7	39	A	83.2	64	A	83.8	89	B	86.5
15	B	85.2	40	B	86.2	65	B	87.0	90	B	87.6
16	B	86.7	41	A	82.9	66	B	86.9	91	A	84.7
17	A	83.1	42	A	83.8	67	B	85.5	92	A	85.1
18	B	85.9	43	A	83.7	68	A	83.7	93	A	83.8
19	B	87.5	44	B	86.6	69	B	86.0	94	B	86.6
20	A	83.8	45	B	85.7	70	A	84.5	95	B	86.7
21	B	87.5	46	A	82.9	71	B	87.9	96	A	84.3
22	A	84.4	47	B	86.9	72	A	82.7	97	A	83.7
23	A	83.4	48	B	86.1	73	A	84.2	98	B	84.9
24	A	84.3	49	B	86.0	74	A	83.9	99	B	85.8
25	B	86.1	50	A	83.8	75	B	85.5	100	B	84.1

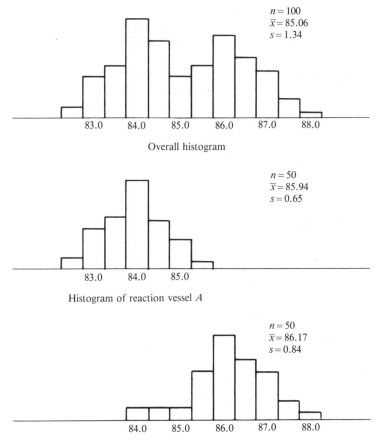

$n = 100$
$\bar{x} = 85.06$
$s = 1.34$

Overall histogram

$n = 50$
$\bar{x} = 85.94$
$s = 0.65$

Histogram of reaction vessel *A*

$n = 50$
$\bar{x} = 86.17$
$s = 0.84$

Histogram of reaction vessel *B*

Figure 5.8   Stratification of Histograms

Exercise 5.1
In a bakery, two bakers, *A* and *B*, are baking bread using two machines (machine 1 and machine 2). The weights of french loaves produced were recorded for 20 days, as shown in Table 5.7. Four loaves were picked randomly from each machine every day and were weighed. The weight specification is 200–225 (g).
1) Make the following histograms:
   a) An overall histogram.

b) A histogram of baker A, and another of baker B.
c) A histogram of machine 1, and another of machine 2.
d) Four histograms showing combinations of different bakers and machines.

2) Study them by comparing them with the specification.

Table 5.7

Day	Baker	Machine 1				Machine 2			
1st	A	209.2	209.5	210.2	212.0	214.3	221.8	214.6	214.4
2nd	A	208.5	208.7	206.2	207.8	215.3	216.7	212.3	212.0
3rd	A	204.2	210.2	210.5	205.9	215.7	213.8	215.2	202.7
4th	B	204.0	203.3	198.2	199.9	212.5	210.2	211.3	210.4
5th	B	209.6	203.7	213.2	209.6	208.4	214.9	212.8	214.8
6th	A	208.1	207.9	211.0	206.2	212.3	216.2	208.4	210.8
7th	A	205.2	204.8	198.7	205.8	208.1	211.9	212.9	209.0
8th	B	199.0	197.7	202.0	213.1	207.5	209.9	210.6	212.3
9th	B	197.2	210.6	199.5	215.3	206.9	207.1	213.6	212.2
10th	B	199.1	207.2	200.8	201.2	209.6	209.5	206.8	214.2
11th	A	204.6	207.0	200.8	204.6	212.2	209.8	207.6	212.6
12th	B	214.7	207.5	205.8	200.9	211.4	211.2	214.4	212.6
13th	B	204.1	196.6	204.6	199.4	209.6	209.2	206.1	207.1
14th	A	200.2	205.5	208.0	202.7	203.5	206.9	210.6	212.3
15th	A	201.1	209.2	205.5	200.0	209.1	206.3	209.8	211.4
16th	A	201.3	203.1	196.3	205.5	208.0	207.9	205.3	203.6
17th	B	202.2	204.4	202.1	206.6	210.0	209.4	209.1	207.0
18th	B	194.1	211.0	208.4	202.6	215.6	211.8	205.4	209.0
19th	B	204.8	201.3	208.4	212.3	214.5	207.5	212.9	204.3
20th	A	200.6	202.3	204.3	201.4	209.1	205.8	212.0	204.2

Chapter 6

Scatter Diagrams

6.1   What Are Scatter Diagrams?

In actual practice, it is often essential to study the relation of two corresponding variables. For example, to what extent will the dimension of a machine part be varied by the change in the speed of a lathe? Or, suppose you would like to control the concentration of a material, and it is preferable to substitute the measurement of concentration by specific gravity, because it is easily measured in practice. To study the relation of two variable such as the speed of the lathe and dimension of a part, or concentration and specific gravity, you can use what is called a *scatter diagram*.

The two variables we will deal with are:
a)   a quality characteristic and a factor affecting it,
b)   two related quality characteristics, or
c)   two factors relating to a single quality characteristic.

In order to grasp the relation between these, it is important, first, to make a scatter diagram and grasp the overall relation.

6.2   How to Make Scatter Diagrams

Scatter diagram is made by the following steps:
Step 1
Collect paired data (x, y), between which you want to study the relations, and arrange the data in a table. It is desirable to have at least 30 pairs of data.
Step 2
Find the maximum and minimum values for both the x and y. Decide the scales of horizontal and vertical axes so that the both lengths become approximately equal, then the diagram will be easier to read.

Keep the number of unit graduations to 3 to 10 for each axis and use round numbers to make it easier to read. When the two variables consist of a factor and a quality characteristic, use the horizontal x-axis for the factor and the vertical y-axis for the quality characteristic.

Step 3
Plot the data on the section paper. When the same data values are obtained from different observations, show these points either by drawing concentric circles, (◉), or plot the second point in the immediate vicinity of the first.

Step 4
Enter all necessary items. Make sure that the following items are included so that anyone besides the maker of the diagram can understand it at a glance:
a) title of the diagram
b) time interval
c) number of pairs of data
d) title and units of each axis
e) name (etc.) of the person who made the diagram.

Example 6.1
A manufacturer of plastic tanks who made them using the blow molding method encountered problems with defective tanks that had thin tank walls. It was suspected that the variation in air pressure, which varied from day to day, was the cause of the nonconforming thin walls. Table 6.1 shows data on blowing air-pressure and percent defective. Let us draw a scatter diagram using this data, according to the steps given above.

Step 1
As seen in Table 6.1, there are 30 pairs of data.
Step 2
In this example, let blowing air-pressure be indicated by x (horizontal axis), and percent defective by y (vertical axis).
Then,
the maximum value of x: x_{max} = 9.4 (kgf/cm^2),
the minimum value of x: x_{min} = 8.2 (kgf/cm^2),
the maximum value of y: y_{max} = 0.928 (%),
the minimum value of y: y_{min} = 0.864 (%).

We mark off
   the horizontal axis in 0.5 (kgf/cm²) intervals, from 8.0 to 9.5
   (kgf/cm²),
and
   the vertical axis in 0.01(%) intervals, from 0.85 to 0.93(%).
Step 3
Plot the data. (See Figure 6.1.)
Step 4
Enter the time interval of the sample obtained (Oct. 1 — Nov. 9),
number of samples ($n = 30$), horizontal axis (blowing air-pressure
[kgf/cm²]), vertical axis (percent defective [%]), and title of
diagram (Scatter diagram of blowing air-pressure and percent
defective).

**Table 6.1   Data of Blowing Air-Pressure and Percent Defective
of Plastic Tank**

Date	Air Pressure (kgf/cm²)	Percent Defective (%)	Date	Air Pressure (kgf/cm²)	Percent Defective (%)
Oct. 1	8.6	0.889	Oct. 22	8.7	0.892
2	8.9	0.884	23	8.5	0.877
3	8.8	0.874	24	9.2	0.885
4	8.8	0.891	25	8.5	0.866
5	8.4	0.874	26	8.3	0.896
8	8.7	0.886	29	8.7	0.896
9	9.2	0.911	30	9.3	0.928
10	8.6	0.912	31	8.9	0.886
11	9.2	0.895	Nov. 1	8.9	0.908
12	8.7	0.896	2	8.3	0.881
15	8.4	0.894	5	8.7	0.882
16	8.2	0.864	6	8.9	0.904
17	9.2	0.922	7	8.7	0.912
18	8.7	0.909	8	9.1	0.925
19	9.4	0.905	9	8.7	0.872

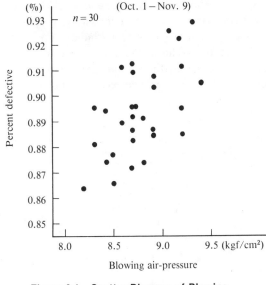

**Figure 6.1 Scatter Diagram of Blowing
Air-Pressure and Percent Defective**

6.3 How to Read Scatter Diagrams

As you can grasp the shape of the distribution in a histogram, the overall distribution of the pairs can be read from a scatter diagram. When doing so, the first thing you should do is to examine whether or not there are any outlying points in the diagram. It can generally be assumed that any such points far from the main group (Figure 6.2) are the result of errors in measurement or recording data, or were caused by some change in the conditions of the operation. It is necessary to exclude these points for the correlation analysis. Yet instead of neglecting these points completely, you should pay due attention to the cause of such irregularities because you often gain unexpected but very useful information by finding out why they occur.

There are many types of scattering patterns, and some typical types are given in Figure 6.3.1 through 6.3.6. In both Figures 6.3.1 and 6.3.2, *y* increases with *x*; this is a *positive correlation*. Also, since Figure 6.3.1 shows this tendency in a very conspicuous way, it is said to be a strong positive correlation. Figures 6.3.4 and 6.3.5 show the opposite of the positive correlation, since as x increases, y decreases; this is called a *negative correlation*. Figure 6.3.4 indicates a strong negative correlation. Figure 6.3.3 shows the case where x and y have no particular relation, so we say there is *no correlation*. In Figure 6.3.6, as x increases, y changes in a curved pattern. This will be explained later.

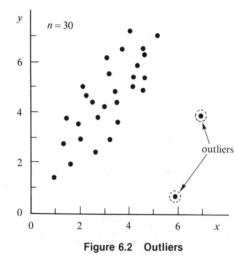

Figure 6.2   Outliers

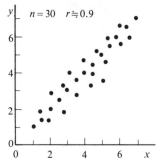

Figure 6.3.1   Positive Correlation

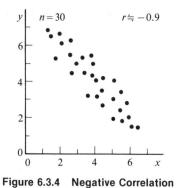

Figure 6.3.4   Negative Correlation

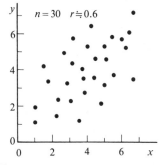

**Figure 6.3.2   Positive Correlation
May Be Present**

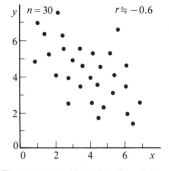

**Figure 6.3.5   Negative Correlation
May Be Present**

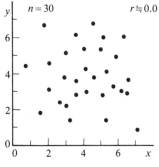

Figure 6.3.3   No Correlation

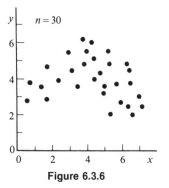

Figure 6.3.6

6.4 Calculation of Correlation Coefficients

To study the relation of x and y, it is important to first draw a scatter diagram; however, in order to understand the strength of the relation in quantitative terms, it is useful to calculate the *correlation coefficient* according to the following definition:

$$r = \frac{S(xy)}{\sqrt{S(xx) \cdot S(yy)}}, \qquad (6.1)$$

where

$$S(xx) = \sum_{i=1}^{n} (x_i - \bar{x})^2 = \sum_{i=1}^{n} x_i^2 - \frac{(\sum_{i=1}^{n} x_i)^2}{n}, \qquad (6.2)$$

$$S(yy) = \sum_{i=1}^{n} (y_i - \bar{y})^2 = \sum_{i=1}^{n} y_i^2 - \frac{(\sum_{i=1}^{n} y_i)^2}{n}, \qquad (6.3)$$

$$S(xy) = \sum_{i=1}^{n} (x_i - \bar{x})(y_i - \bar{y})$$

$$= \sum_{i=1}^{n} x_i y_i - \frac{(\sum_{i=1}^{n} x_i) \cdot (\sum_{i=1}^{n} y_i)}{n}. \qquad (6.4)$$

"n" is the number of pairs of data, and $S(xy)$ is called *covariation*. The correlation coefficient, r, is in the range $-1 \leq r \leq 1$. If the absolute value of r is greater than 1, there has clearly been a miscalculation, and you should recalculate. In the case of strong positive correlation such as in Figure 6.3.1, it attains a value near $+1$, and likewise, with a strong negative correlation as in Figure 6.3.4, it is close to -1. That is, when $|r|$ is near 1, it indicates a strong correlation between x and y, and when $|r|$ is close to 0, a weak correlation. Further, when $|r| = 1$, the data will show up in a straight line. If you keep this in mind and makes a habit of estimating the value of r from the scatter diagram, you can check miscalculation.

Let us calculate the correlation coefficient for the previous example of the plastic tanks. A supplemental table of calculations is in Table 6.2. From this, we have

$$S(xx) = \Sigma x_i^2 - \frac{(\Sigma x_i)^2}{n} = 2312.02 - \frac{263.2^2}{30} = 2.88, \quad (6.5)$$

$$S(yy) = \Sigma y_i^2 - \frac{(\Sigma y_i)^2}{n} = 23.97833 - \frac{26.816^2}{30}$$

$$= 0.00840, \quad (6.6)$$

$$S(xy) = \Sigma x_i y_i - \frac{(\Sigma x_i)(\Sigma y_i)}{n}$$

$$= 235.3570 - \frac{263.2 \times 26.816}{30} = 0.0913, \quad (6.7)$$

$$r = \frac{0.0913}{\sqrt{2.88 \times 0.00840}} = 0.59. \quad (6.8)$$

The value of r is 0.59, so there is a positive correlation between blowing air-pressure and percent defective of plastic tanks.

Table 6.2

Date	x	y	x^2	y^2	xy
Oct. 1	8.6	0.889	73.96	0.79032	7.6454
2	8.9	0.884	79.21	0.78146	7.8676
3	8.8	0.874	77.44	0.76388	7.6912
4	8.8	0.891	77.44	0.79388	7.8408
5	8.4	0.874	70.56	0.76388	7.3416
8	8.7	0.886	75.69	0.78500	7.7082
9	9.2	0.911	84.64	0.82992	8.3812
10	8.6	0.912	73.96	0.83174	7.8432
11	9.2	0.895	84.64	0.80102	8.2340
12	8.7	0.896	75.69	0.80282	7.7952
15	8.4	0.894	70.56	0.79924	7.5096
16	8.2	0.864	67.24	0.74650	7.0848
17	9.2	0.922	84.64	0.85008	8.4824
18	8.7	0.909	75.69	0.82628	7.9083
19	9.4	0.905	88.36	0.81902	8.5070
22	8.7	0.892	75.69	0.79566	7.7604
23	8.5	0.877	72.25	0.76913	7.4545
24	9.2	0.885	84.64	0.78322	8.1420
25	8.5	0.866	72.25	0.74996	7.3610
26	8.3	0.896	68.89	0.80282	7.4368
29	8.7	0.896	75.69	0.80282	7.7952
30	9.3	0.928	86.49	0.86118	8.6304
31	8.9	0.886	79.21	0.78500	7.8854
Nov. 1	8.9	0.908	79.21	0.82446	8.0812
2	8.3	0.881	68.89	0.77616	7.3123
5	8.7	0.882	75.69	0.77792	7.6734
6	8.9	0.904	79.21	0.81722	8.0456
7	8.7	0.912	75.69	0.83174	7.9344
8	9.1	0.925	82.81	0.85562	8.4175
9	8.7	0.872	75.69	0.76038	7.5864
Total	263.2	26.816	2312.02	23.97833	235.3570

6.5 Notes on Correlation Analysis

The method of judging the existence of correlation by making a scatter diagram and calculating the correlation coefficient, as described above, is called *correlation analysis*. Some comments concerning correlation analysis are given here in sections (1) through (4).

(1) Coordinate Axes

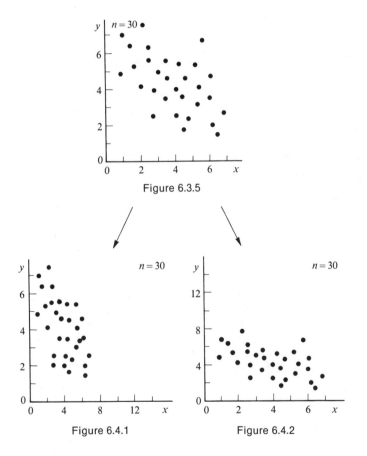

Figure 6.3.5

Figure 6.4.1

Figure 6.4.2

Figure 6.4 Visual Effect of Coordinate Scaling

In Step 2 of drawing the scatter diagram, explanation was given regarding the drawing of coordinate axes. The same pairs of data are plotted in Figure 6.4. The scale of the horizontal axis in Figure 6.4.1 is 1/2 of that of Figure 6.3.5, and the vertical axis of Figure 6.4.2 is 1/2 of that of Figure 6.3.5. It was possible to interpret the distribution of Figure 6.3.5 as a negative correlation, but this is not so clear in either Figure 6.4.1 or Figure 6.4.2; it may even appear to show no correlation. In this way, if the scale is poorly set, it will result in erroneous interpretation of information. Thus we must draw the coordinate axes properly as shown in Step 2.

(2) Stratification

Both Figure 6.5.1 and Figure 6.5.2 show the relation between the amount of impurity and the viscosity of a manufactured substance in scatter diagrams. In Figure 6.5.1, when Company A's and Company B's data are combined indiscriminately, there appears to be no correlation (Figure 6.5.1, left); but when distinguished as in Figure 6.5.1, right, a clear correlation becomes apparent. On the other hand Figure 6.5.2. seems to show an overall correlation, but when stratified into A and B (Figure 6.5.2, right), the correlation disappears. When there is a stratification factor, you can obtain vital information by distinguishing the data of different strata by different colors or symbols. For this purpose, you should take care always to keep a record of the data's origin and background which will become a useful information for analysis afterward.

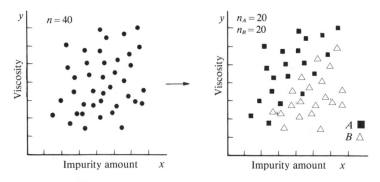

Figure 6.5.1   Stratification in Scatter Diagram

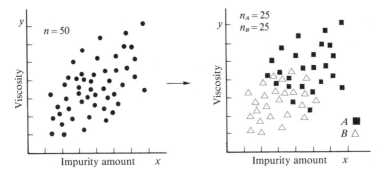

Figure 6.5.2 Stratification in Scatter Diagram

(3) Ranges of Variables

Figure 6.6.1 and Figure 6.6.2 are two halves of Figure 6.3.6, divided by taking $0 \leq x \leq 4$ for Figure 6.6.1 and $4 < x \leq 8$ for Figure 6.6.2. In Section 6.3, it was noted that as x increases, y changes with a curved pattern. If you examined this with $0 \leq x \leq 4$, you would probably say that there is a positive correlation, as seen in Figure 6.6.1. On the other hand, in the case of Figure 6.6.2, you would see a negative correlation.

Figure 6.7.1 is the part of Figure 6.3.2 from $3 \leq x \leq 6$ only. There was a clear positive correlation in Figure 6.3.2; but in Figure 6.7.1 there was no noticeable correlation. As seen in these examples, examining whether there is a correlation or not greatly depends on the range of variables and it does not necessarily arise same in all ranges. The same thing also holds true for the case with different strata. Figure 6.5.2 shows the relationship between the amount of impurity and viscosity with two lots of A and B. There is a correlation when lot A and lot B data are mixed, but when these are separated, there is no correlation between these. As it is extremely dangerous to extrapolate a conclusion beyond the data that was obtained, in this case, you should either verify through experiments or carry out an adequate technical investigation.

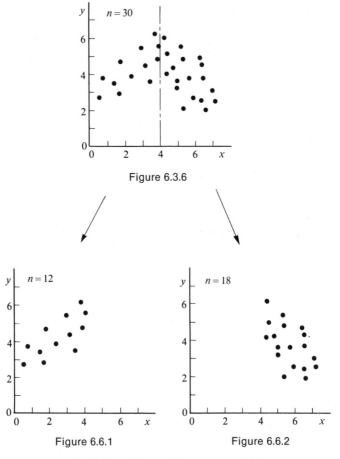

Figure 6.3.6

Figure 6.6.1   Figure 6.6.2

Figure 6.6   Effect of Range of Variable (1)

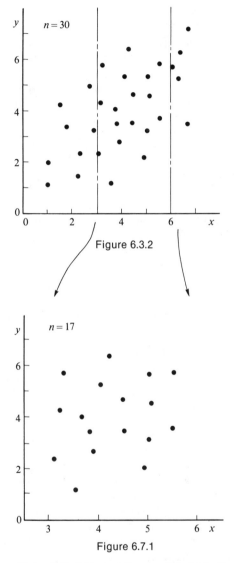

Figure 6.3.2

Figure 6.7.1

Figure 6.7   Effect of Range of Variable (2)

(4) False Correlations

According to a certain survey, there was a strong positive correlation between the consumer prices index and the number of incidents of fires. If so, then, if consumer prices index lowers, will there be indeed fewer fire emergencies? The answer is most likely "No." In order to reduce the incidence of fires, we would stress the importance of cleaning-up of ashtrays and not to discard any trash that would bring upon incendiary. In this way, when calculating a correlation coefficient between two variables, it is sometimes found, by chance, there is a high value of correlation coefficient between the two variables which originally have little or no cause-and-effect relationship to each other. This sort of correlation is called a *false correlation*. Even if the correlation coefficient is high, it does not necessarily indicate a cause-and-effect relationship. It is necessary to take good note of this fact, and to think about its meaning in science and technology.

6.6   What Is Regression Analysis?

In the previous example of the plastic tanks with defective thin walls, we found that there was a positive correlation between blowing air-pressure and percent defective. In order to prevent this problem of thin walls, we must carry out our analysis one step further. When the blowing air-pressure is at a certain value, how thick will the walls be formed? How should the air pressure be controlled so that the walls of the tanks do not become thin? To realize this analysis and answer the questions, it is necessary to comprehend the relation between the blowing air-pressure and the wall thickness quantitatively.

Table 6.3 shows data from an experiment in which the air pressure was changed and the thickness of the tank walls was measured each time. Figure 6.8 is a scatter diagram based on the data. From this diagram, it would seem that air pressure and wall thickness had a straight-line relation. Now, let us denote air pressure by x and wall thickness by y, and assume a straight-line relation;

$$y = \alpha + \beta x$$

Such a straight line is generally called a *regression line*, where y is the response variable (or dependent variable), and x is the explanatory (or independent) variable. Also, α is called a *constant* and β is called a *regression coefficient*. The quantitative way of grasping the relation between x and y by seeking a regression form of x and y is called *regression analysis*.

Table 6.3

Air pressure (kgf/cm²)	8.0	8.5	9.0	9.5	10.0
Wall thickness (mm)	4.62	4.12	3.21	2.86	1.83
	4.50	3.88	3.05	2.53	2.02
	4.43	4.01	3.16	2.71	2.24
	4.81	3.67	3.30	2.62	1.95

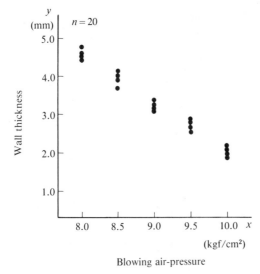

Figure 6.8   Relationship Between Air Pressure and Thickness

6.7   Estimation of Regression Lines

Let $(x_i \, y_i)$ $(1 \leq i \leq n)$ be a set of n pairs of observed data. Let $\hat{\alpha}$ and $\hat{\beta}$ be the estimated value of α and β, and let e_i be the residual between y_i and $\hat{\alpha} + \hat{\beta}x_i$, that is

$$e_i = y_i - (\hat{\alpha} + \hat{\beta}x_i) \quad (1 \leq i \leq n). \tag{6.9}$$

By the *least squares method*, $\hat{\alpha}$ and $\hat{\beta}$ are obtained as the values which minimize $\sum_{i=1}^{n} e_i^2$, the sum of squares of residuals. This method is done by the following steps.

Step 1
Obtain $\bar{x}$ and $\bar{y}$ from the data.

Step 2
Calculate $S(xx)$ and $S(xy)$.

Step 3
$\hat{\beta}$ is obtained from

$$\hat{\beta} = \frac{S(xy)}{S(xx)}, \tag{6.10}$$

and
$\hat{\alpha}$ is obtained from

$$\hat{\alpha} = \bar{y} - \hat{\beta}\bar{x}. \tag{6.11}$$

The values of $\hat{\alpha}$ and $\hat{\beta}$ obtained by these steps make the sum of squares of residuals minimum.

Now, using the data in Table 6.3, let us calculate the regression line:

Step 1

$$\bar{x} = (8.0 + 8.5 + 9.0 + 9.5 + 10.0) \times 4/20 = 9.00 \tag{6.12}$$
$$\bar{y} = (4.62 + 4.50 + \cdots + 1.95)/20 = 3.276 \tag{6.13}$$

Step 2

$$S(xx) = \Sigma x_i^2 - (\Sigma x_i)^2/n = 1630 - 180^2/20 = 10.0 \quad (6.14)$$
$$S(xy) = \Sigma x_i y_i - (\Sigma x_i) \cdot (\Sigma y_i)/n$$
$$= 576.88 - 180 \times 65.52/20 = -12.8 \quad\quad (6.15)$$

Step 3

$$\hat{\beta} = -12.8/10.0 = -1.28 \quad\quad\quad (6.16)$$
$$\hat{\alpha} = 3.276 - (-1.28) \times 9.00 = 14.80 \quad\quad (6.17)$$

Thus, the regression line is expressed by $y = 14.80 - 1.28x$. That is, for every 1 kgf/cm² increase of the air pressure, the wall thickness decreases by 1.28 mm.

Figure 6.9 shows the regression line calculated above. The points on the scatter diagram should mostly be evenly distributed around the regression line. If not, there may be a miscalculation and those steps should be checked.

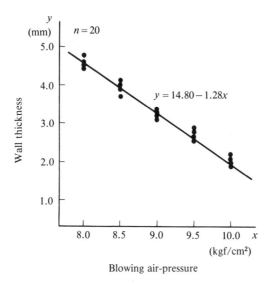

Figure 6.9   Relationship Between Air Pressure and Thickness

6.8 Notes on Regression Analysis

Some comments concerning scatter diagrams and correlation analysis also apply to regression analysis. What is particularly important is that you should never carry out regression analysis without first drawing a scatter diagram.

Look at the scatter diagrams in Figures 6.10.1 through 6.10.4 (Figure 6.10). They depict four sets of raw data. These four graphs, taken from F. J. Anscombe's *Graphs in Statistical Analysis*, yield almost the same results when subjected to regression analysis (See Table 6.4). However, you can see that their point distributions of scatter diagram are completely different from one another. The diagram in Figure 6.10.1 looks as though it could be used almost just as it is as a regression line, but in Figure 6.10.2 , a curved line should be fitted and it is unnatural to apply a straight line. Also, in Figure 6.10.3, there is one outlying point, so you should probably either ignore it or repeat the measurements again. Of the 11 sets of data in Figure 6.10.4, the point $x=19$ has a great influence in the determination of the line, but since there are only data for $x=8$ or 19, it would be better to get more data. These types of phenomena can only be clearly understood by drawing a scatter diagram. Though a regression line can be calculated using any kind of data, it is actually incautious to calculate a regression line without drawing a scatter diagram.

For either correlation analysis or regression analysis, the starting point is a scatter diagram. You should never forget that the first step is to examine the data carefully.

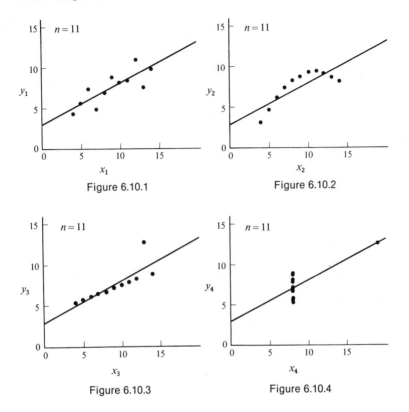

Figure 6.10.1

Figure 6.10.2

Figure 6.10.3

Figure 6.10.4

Figure 6.10   Various Scatter Diagrams Having the Same Regression Line

Table 6.4   Example*

No.	x_1	y_1	x_2	y_2	x_3	y_3	x_4	y_4
1	10	8.04	10	9.14	10	7.46	8	6.58
2	8	6.95	8	8.14	8	6.77	8	5.76
3	13	7.58	13	8.74	13	12.74	8	7.71
4	9	8.81	9	8.77	9	7.11	8	8.84
5	11	8.33	11	9.26	11	7.81	8	8.47
6	14	9.96	14	8.10	14	8.84	8	7.04
7	6	7.24	6	6.13	6	6.08	8	5.25
8	4	4.26	4	3.10	4	5.39	19	12.50
9	12	10.84	12	9.13	12	8.15	8	5.56
10	7	4.82	7	7.26	7	6.42	8	7.91
11	5	5.68	5	4.74	5	5.73	8	6.89
$\bar{x}$	9.0		9.0		9.0		9.0	
$\bar{y}$	7.50		7.50		7.50		7.50	
$S(xx)$	110.0		110.0		110.0		110.0	
$S(yy)$	41.27		41.27		41.23		41.23	
$S(xy)$	55.01		55.00		54.97		54.99	

* Anscombe, F.J., Graphs in Statistical Analysis, *American Statistician*, **27**,17-21 (1973)

Exercise 6.1

The data below shows carbon content x (%) and tensile strength y (kg/mm²) of a certain steel.

1) Make a scatter diagram and read it.
2) Obtain correlation coefficient r.
3) Obtain a regression line which estimates the tensile strength y from the carbon content x.

No.	x (%)	y (kg/mm²)
1	2.0	43
2	2.4	46
3	2.2	45
4	2.3	44
5	2.5	45
6	2.8	48
7	2.2	43
8	2.7	47
9	2.4	44
10	2.3	45
11	2.0	42
12	2.2	44
13	2.6	47
14	2.1	44
15	2.5	46
16	2.7	47
17	2.1	42
18	2.6	48
19	2.4	45
20	2.1	43
21	2.3	45
22	2.2	43
23	2.3	46
24	2.4	47
25	2.3	44
26	2.4	45
27	2.6	46
28	2.5	42
29	2.6	46
30	2.4	46

Chapter 7

Control Charts

7.1 What Are Control Charts?

A control chart was first proposed in 1924 by W.A. Shewhart, who belonged to the Bell Telephone Laboratories, with a view to eliminating an abnormal variation by distinguishing variations due to *assignable causes* from those due to *chance causes*. A control chart consists of a central line, a pair of control limits, one each, allocated above and below the central line, and characteristic values plotted on the chart which represent the state of a process. If all these values are plotted within the control limits without any particular tendency, the process is regarded as being in the controlled state. However, if they fall outside the control limits or show a peculiar form, the process is judged to be out of control. Examples are shown in Figure 7.1.

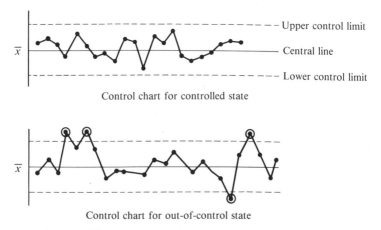

Control chart for controlled state

Control chart for out-of-control state

Figure 7.1 Examples of Control Charts

The quality of a product manufactured in a process is inevitably accompanied by variation. Various causes of such variation exist and they can be classified into the following two types.

Chance cause
Variation by chance cause is unavoidable and inevitably occurs in a process, even if the operation is carried out using standardized raw materials and methods. It is not practical to eliminate the chance cause technically and economically for the present.

Assignable cause
Variation by assignable cause means that there are meaningful factors to be investigated. It is avoidable and cannot be overlooked: there are cases caused by not following certain standards or applying improper standards.

When points fall outside the control limits or show a particular tendency, we say a process is *out of control*, and this is equivalent to saying, "There exist assignable causes of variation, and the process is not in the controlled state." In order to control a process, it is their recurrence, while allowing variations by chance causes.

To make a control chart it is necessary to estimate the variation by chance causes. For this purpose we divide data into *subgroups* within which the lot of raw materials, machines, operators and other factors are common, so that the variation within a subgroup can be regarded approximately the same as the variation by chance causes.

There are various types of control chart, according to the characteristic values or purpose. In any type of control chart the control limit is calculated by the formula:

$$\text{(average value)} \pm 3 \times \text{(standard deviation)},$$

where the standard deviation is that of variation due to chance causes. This type of control chart is called a 3-sigma control chart.

7.2 Types of Control Chart

There are two types of control chart, the one for continuous value and the other for discrete value. The types of chart prescribed by JIS are shown in Table 7.1 and their control lines are shown in Table 7.2.

Table 7.1 Types of Control Chart

Characteristic Value	Name
Continuous value	$\bar{x}$-R chart (average value and range) x chart (measured value)
Discrete value	pn chart (number of defective units) p chart (fraction defective) c chart (number of defects) u chart (number of defects per unit)

Table 7.2 List of Formulas for Control Lines

Type of Control Chart	Upper Control Limit (UCL), Central Line (CL), Lower Control Limit (LCL)
$\bar{x}$	$\begin{aligned} \text{UCL} &= \bar{\bar{x}} + A_2\bar{R} \\ \text{CL} &= \bar{\bar{x}} \\ \text{LCL} &= \bar{\bar{x}} - A_2\bar{R} \end{aligned}$
R	$\begin{aligned} \text{UCL} &= D_4\bar{R} \\ \text{CL} &= \bar{R} \\ \text{LCL} &= D_3\bar{R} \end{aligned}$
x	$\begin{aligned} \text{UCL} &= \bar{x} + 2.66\bar{R}s \\ \text{CL} &= \bar{x} \\ \text{LCL} &= \bar{x} - 2.66\bar{R}s \end{aligned}$
pn	$\begin{aligned} \text{UCL} &= \bar{p}n + 3\sqrt{\bar{p}n(1 - \bar{p})} \\ \text{CL} &= \bar{p}n \\ \text{LCL} &= \bar{p}n - 3\sqrt{\bar{p}n(1 - \bar{p})} \end{aligned}$
p	$\begin{aligned} \text{UCL} &= \bar{p} + 3\sqrt{\bar{p}(1 - \bar{p})/n} \\ \text{CL} &= \bar{p} \\ \text{LCL} &= \bar{p} - 3\sqrt{\bar{p}(1 - \bar{p})/n} \end{aligned}$
c	$\begin{aligned} \text{UCL} &= \bar{c} + 3\sqrt{\bar{c}} \\ \text{CL} &= \bar{c} \\ \text{LCL} &= \bar{c} - 3\sqrt{\bar{c}} \end{aligned}$
u	$\begin{aligned} \text{UCL} &= \bar{u} + 3\sqrt{\bar{u}/n} \\ \text{CL} &= \bar{u} \\ \text{LCL} &= \bar{u} - 3\sqrt{\bar{u}/n} \end{aligned}$

(1) $\bar{x}$-R Chart

This is used for controlling and analyzing a process using continuous values of product quality such as length, weight or concentration and this provides the larger amount of information on the process. $\bar{x}$ represents an average value of a subgroup and R represents the range of the subgroup. An R chart is used usually in combination with an $\bar{x}$ chart to control the variation within a subgroup.

(2) x Chart

When the data on a process is obtained at a long interval or subgrouping of data is not effective, the data is plotted as each and this can be used as a control chart. Since there is no subgroup and the R value cannot be calculated, the moving range Rs of successive data is used for the calculation of control limits of x.

(3) pn Chart, p Chart

These charts are used when the quality characteristic is represented by the number of defective units or fraction defective. For a sample of constant size, a pn chart of the number of defective units is used, whereas a p chart of the fraction defective is used for a sample of varying size.

(4) c Chart, u Chart

These are used for controlling and analyzing a process by defects of a product, such as scratches on plated metal, number of defective solderings inside a TV set or unevenly woven texture of fabrics. A c chart of the number of defects is used for a product of constant size, while a u chart is used for a product of varying size.

7.3 How to Make Control Charts

(1) $\bar{x}$-R Chart

Procedure	Example

Step 1 Collect data

Collect approximately 100 data. Divide them into 20 to 25 subgroups with 4 to 5 in each, making each of them uniform within the subgroup. Fill a data sheet with them (Table 7.3). When there is no technical reason for subgrouping, divide the data in the order they are obtained. The size of a group is usually between 2 and 10 in most cases.

Table 7.3 Data Sheet for $\bar{x}$-R Chart

Subgroup No.	x_1	x_2	x_3	x_4	x_5	Σx	$\bar{x}$	R
1	47	32	44	35	20	178	35.6	27
2	19	37	31	25	34	146	29.2	18

						Total	$\bar{X}$	R
3	19	11	16	11	44	101	20.2	33
4	29	29	42	59	38	197	39.4	30
5	28	12	45	36	25	146	29.2	33
6	40	35	11	38	33	157	31.4	29
7	15	30	12	33	26	116	23.2	21
8	35	44	32	11	38	160	32.0	33
9	27	37	26	20	35	145	29.0	17
10	23	45	26	37	32	163	32.6	22
11	28	44	40	31	18	161	32.2	26
12	31	25	24	32	22	134	26.8	10
13	22	37	19	47	14	139	27.8	33
14	37	32	12	38	30	149	29.8	26
15	25	40	24	50	19	158	31.6	31
16	7	31	23	18	32	111	22.2	25
17	38	0	41	40	37	156	31.2	41
18	35	12	29	48	20	144	28.8	36
19	31	20	35	24	47	157	31.4	27
20	12	27	38	40	31	148	29.6	28
21	52	42	52	24	25	195	39.0	28
22	20	31	15	3	28	97	19.4	28
23	29	47	41	32	22	171	34.2	25
24	28	27	22	32	54	163	32.6	32
25	42	34	15	29	21	141	28.2	27
Total							746.6	686
Average							$\bar{\bar{X}}=$ 29.86	$\bar{R}=$ 27.44

Step 2 Calculate $\bar{x}$'s

Calculate the average value $\bar{x}$ for each subgroup.

$$\bar{x} = \frac{x_1 + x_2 + \cdots + x_n}{n}$$

where n is the size of a subgroup.

The result is generally calculated to one decimal place more than that of the original data.

Step 3 Calculate $\bar{\bar{x}}$

Calculate the gross average $\bar{\bar{x}}$ by dividing the total of $\bar{x}$'s of each subgroup by the number of subgroups k.

$$\bar{\bar{x}} = \frac{\bar{x}_1 + \bar{x}_2 + \cdots + \bar{x}_k}{k}$$

$\bar{\bar{x}}$ should be calculated to two decimal places more than that of the measured value.

Step 4 Calculate R

Calculate the range of each subgroup R by subtracting the minimum value from the maximum value of the data in a subgroup.

$R =$ (maximum value in a subgroup)
   $-$ (minimum value in a subgroup)

Step 2

As for the first group,

$$\bar{x} = (47 + 32 + 44 + 35 + 20)/5 = 35.6$$

Step 3

$$\bar{\bar{x}} = (35.6 + 29.2 + \cdots + 28.2)/25 = 29.86$$

Step 4

For the first group,

$$R = 47 - 20 = 27$$

Step 5 Calculate $\overline{R}$

Calculate the average $\overline{R}$ of the Range R, by dividing the total of the R's of each subgroup by the number of groups k.

$$\overline{R} = \frac{R_1 + R_2 + \cdots + R_k}{k}$$

$\overline{R}$ should be calculated to two decimal places more than that of the measured value (the same decimal place as that of $\overline{\overline{x}}$).

Step 6 Calculate the control lines

Calculate each of the control lines for the $\overline{x}$ chart and the R chart by the following formulas.

$\overline{x}$ chart

Central line:
$$CL = \overline{\overline{x}}$$

Upper control limit:
$$UCL = \overline{\overline{x}} + A_2\overline{R}$$

Lower control limit:
$$LCL = \overline{\overline{x}} - A_2\overline{R}$$

Step 5

$$\overline{R} = (27 + 18 + \cdots + 27)/25 = 27.44$$

Step 6

$\overline{x}$ chart

$$CL = \overline{\overline{x}} = 29.86$$

$$UCL = \overline{\overline{x}} + A_2\overline{R}$$
$$= 29.86 + 0.577 \times 27.44 = 45.69$$

$$LCL = \overline{\overline{x}} - A_2\overline{R}$$
$$= 29.86 - 0.577 \times 27.44 = 14.03$$

R chart
Central line:
$$CL = \bar{R}$$
Upper control limit:
$$UCL = D_4\bar{R}$$
Lower control limit:
$$LCL = D_3\bar{R}$$

LCL is not considered when n is smaller than 6.

A_2, D_4 and D_3 are the coefficients determined by the size of a subgroup (n), and are shown in Table 7.4 and also in Table A.2 of the Appendix.

R chart

$$CL = \bar{R} = 27.44$$

$$UCL = D_4\bar{R} = 2.115 \times 27.44 = 58.04$$

$$LCL = \text{—— (not considered)}$$

Table 7.4   List of Coefficients for $\bar{x}$-R Chart

Size of Subgroup	$\bar{x}$ Chart	R Chart		
n	A_2	D_3	D_4	d_2
2	1.880	—	3.267	1.128
3	1.023	—	2.575	1.693
4	0.729	—	2.282	2.059
5	0.577	—	2.115	2.326
6	0.483	—	2.004	2.534

Step 7 Draw the control lines

First, prepare a sheet of squared paper and mark the left-hand vertical axis with the values of $\bar{x}$ and R and the horizontal axis with the subgroup number. Assign the upper control limit and lower control limit at a width of 20 to 30 mm. Draw a solid line for the central line and a dotted line for both of the control limits.

Step 8 Plot the points

Mark the $\bar{x}$ and R values of each subgroup on the same vertical line in the order of subgroup number. Mark the subgroup number on the horizontal line at intervals of 2 to 5 mm. Put ● marks for $\bar{x}$ and × marks for R for easy recognition and circle them for values outside the limits.

Step 9 Write necessary items

Write the size of subgroup (n) in the upper left-hand corner of the $\bar{x}$ chart. Write in also other necessary items relevant to the process, such as the names of the process and product, period, measuring method, work conditions, shift, etc.

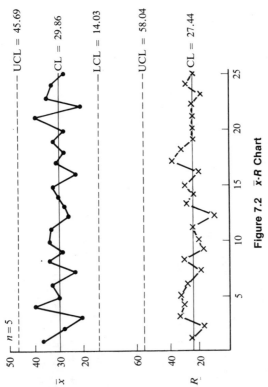

Figure 7.2 $\bar{x}$-R Chart

(2) *pn* Chart

Procedure	Example
Step 1 Collect data Take a sample and classify the product quality into conforming and non-conforming units, according to the inspection standard. In this case take a sample of such size that between 1 and 5 non-conforming units on the average are included within a subgroup, and gather 20 to 25 such subgroups (Table 7.5).	

Table 7.5   Data Sheet for *pn* Chart

Subgroup No.	Size of Subgroup n	pn (Number of Defective Units)
1	100	4
2	100	2
3	100	0
4	100	5
5	100	3
6	100	2
7	100	4
8	100	3
9	100	2
10	100	6
11	100	1
12	100	4
13	100	1
14	100	0
15	100	2
16	100	3
17	100	1
18	100	6
19	100	1
20	100	3
21	100	3
22	100	2
23	100	0
24	100	7
25	100	3
Total	$\Sigma n = 2500$	$\Sigma pn = 68$

Step 2 Calculate $\bar{p}$

Calculate the average fraction defective $\bar{p}$ by dividing the total number of defective units for each subgroup by the total number of samples.

$$\bar{p} = \frac{\Sigma pn}{k \times n}$$

Step 3 Calculate the control lines

Central line:

$$CL = \bar{p}n$$

Upper control limit:

$$UCL = \bar{p}n + 3\sqrt{\bar{p}n\,(1-\bar{p})}$$

Lower control limit:

$$LCL = \bar{p}n - 3\sqrt{\bar{p}n\,(1-\bar{p})}$$

LCL is not considered when its value becomes a negative number.

Step 4 Construct the control chart

Mark the horizontal axis with the subgroup number and the vertical axis with the number of defective units. Draw a solid line for the central line pn and dotted lines for UCL and LCL. Then plot the number of defective units of each subgroup.

Step 2

$$\bar{p} = \frac{\Sigma pn}{k \times n} = \frac{68}{25 \times 100} = 0.0272$$

Step 3

$$
\begin{aligned}
CL &= \bar{p}n = 0.0272 \times 100 = 2.72 \\
UCL &= \bar{p}n + 3\sqrt{\bar{p}n(1-\bar{p})} \\
&= 2.72 + 3\sqrt{2.72 \times (1 - 0.0272)} = 7.60 \\
LCL &= \bar{p}n - 3\sqrt{\bar{p}n(1-\bar{p})} \\
&= 2.72 - 3\sqrt{2.72 \times (1 - 0.0272)} \\
&= \text{---}\ (\text{not considered})
\end{aligned}
$$

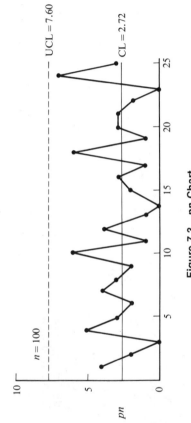

Figure 7.3 *pn* Chart

7.4 How to Read Control Charts

What is most important in process control is to grasp the state of process accurately by reading a control chart and take appropriate actions promptly when anything unusual in the process is found. The controlled state of a process is the state in which the process is stable and the process average and variation do not change. Whether a process is in the controlled state or not is judged by the following criteria from the control chart.

1) Out of control limits
Points which are outside the control limits.

2) Run
Run is the state in which points occur continually on one side of the central line and the number of points is called the length of *run*.
   Seven-point length of run is considered as abnormal.
   Even if the length of run is under 6 the following cases are considered to be abnormal.
a) At least 10 out of 11 consecutive points occur on one side of the central line.
b) At least 12 out of 14 consecutive points occur on one side of the central line.
c) At least 16 out of 20 consecutive points occur on one side of the central line.

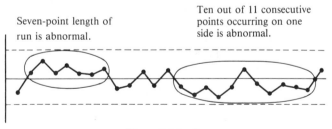

Seven-point length of run is abnormal.

Ten out of 11 consecutive points occurring on one side is abnormal.

Figure 7.4.1   Run

3) Trend

When the points form a continuous upward or downward curve, this is said to have a trend.

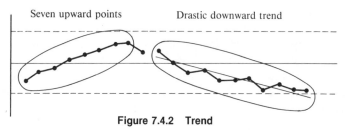

Seven upward points   Drastic downward trend

Figure 7.4.2   Trend

4) Approach to the control limits

Considering points which approach the 3-sigma control limits, if 2 out of 3 points occur outside of the 2-sigma lines, this case is considered to be abnormal.

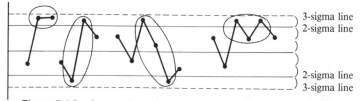

3-sigma line
2-sigma line

2-sigma line
3-sigma line

Figure 7.4.3   Approach to the Control Limits (2 out of 3 points)

5) Approach to the central line

When most of the points are arranged within the central 1.5-sigma lines (the bisectors of the central line and each of the control limits), this is due to an inappropriate way of subgrouping. Approach to the central line does not mean a controlled state, but it means mixing of data with a different population in subgroups, which make the width of control limits too wide. At this situation it is necessary to change the way of subgrouping.

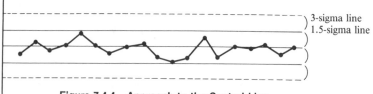

3-sigma line
1.5-sigma line

Figure 7.4.4   Approach to the Central Line

6) Periodicity
When the curve repeatedly shows an up-and-down trend for the almost same interval, this is also abnormal.

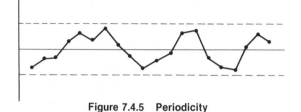

Figure 7.4.5   Periodicity

7.5   Process Analysis by Control Charts

The objective of *process analysis* can be defined as identifying specific assignable causes of variation of a quality characteristic in a process. After finding such assignable causes through the process analysis, it is necessary to conduct a series of remedical actions to the assignable causes.

(1) Subgrouping

Subgrouping is the most important part in the preparation of a control chart and it determines its performance. Improper subgrouping leads to a useless chart.

After the quality characteristic of a process to be analyzed or controlled is decided, the data will be collected. Variation of a quality characteristic in a process arises from various causes. Accordingly, prior to subgrouping, it is necessary to consider the variation to be eliminated, and then try to group the data in such a way that the variation by permissible factors constitutes the within-subgroup variation. For this purpose,

a) Operation should be carried out under nearly the same conditions (from technical point of view).

b) Data collected in a comparatively short period should be grouped together.

The following points should be considered in subgrouping.
a) There are various ways of subgrouping. You should change the size of subgroup and try various ways of combining data.
b) Change in the way of subgrouping will cause a change in the factors constituting within-subgroup variation.

A control chart cannot be used effectively without knowing the components of within-subgroup variation. The following example shows how the components of the within-subgroup variation change, depending upon the way of subgrouping.

Example 7.1

In a machining process a dimension of a part is used as a control characteristic of the process. The main factors affecting the dimension are the quality of raw materials, shape of the cutting tool and adjustment of the tools for abrasion. The process conditions are as follows:
a) One lot of raw materials corresponds to one week's working.
b) The cutting tools undergo grinding everyday.
c) The tools should be adjusted at the beginning of morning and afternoon shifts.

In this case variation within one adjustment is regarded as permissible and the criteria for control will be whether the adjustment is carried out correctly and the tools provided are in normal condition. Then the data should be grouped in such a way that variation within one adjustment becomes a within-subgroup variation and variation between adjustments becomes a between-subgroup variation.

Table 7.6 shows the data sheet, Tables 7.7 and 7.8 show the way of subgrouping and Table 7.9 shows the components of within-subgroup and between-subgroup variations, respectively.

Table 7.6 Data Sheet

Date		Data	n	Remarks		
Dec. 1	a.m.	39	39	adjustment	Tool	
	p.m.	40	42	adjustment	No. 1	
Dec. 2	a.m.	42	41	adjustment	Tool	Raw material
	p.m.	43	42	adjustment	No. 2	Lot No. 1
Dec. 3	a.m.	38	37	adjustment	Tool	
	p.m.	38	38	adjustment	No. 3	

Table 7.7   Subgrouping of $n=2$

Date		Data	
Dec. 1	a.m.	(39	39)
	p.m.	(40	42)
Dec. 2	a.m.	(42	41)
	p.m.	(43	42)
Dec. 3	a.m.	(38	37)
	p.m.	(38	38)

Table 7.8   Subgrouping of $n=4$

Date		Data	
Dec. 1	a.m.	(39	39)
	p.m.	(40	42)
Dec. 2	a.m.	(42	41)
	p.m.	(43	42)
Dec. 3	a.m.	(38	37)
	p.m.	(38	38)

Table 7.9   Components of Within-Subgroup and Between-Subgroup Variations by Subgrouping of Tables 7.7 and 7.8

	Table 7.7 Subgrouping of $n=2$	Table 7.8 Subgrouping of $n=4$
Within-subgroup variation	Measuring error Sampling error Process variation within adjustment	Measuring error Sampling error Process variation within and between adjustments
Between-subgroup variation	Between adjustments Between days Between tools Between materials	Between days Between tools Between materials

(2) Within-Subgroup Variation and Between-Subgroup Variation

Variation of data is classified as within-subgroup variation and between-subgroup variation. The former is the variation which appears in a subgroup and is found from the $\bar{R}$ value of a R chart. On the other hand, between-subgroup variation is the one which appears between subgroups and is found from the distribution of the $\bar{x}$ points on an $\bar{x}$ chart.

Let the variance within a subgroup be $\sigma_w{}^2$ and the variance between subgroups be $\sigma_b{}^2$, then

$$\sigma_{\bar{x}}{}^2 = \sigma_b{}^2 + \frac{\sigma_w{}^2}{n}, \tag{7.1}$$

where $\sigma_{\bar{x}}{}^2$ is the variance of $\bar{x}$. σ_w is estimated from $\bar{R}$ by

$$\hat{\sigma}_w = \bar{R}/d_2, \tag{7.2}$$

where d_2 is a coefficient which depends on the size of subgroup, n, and shown in Table 7.4. Here, the superscript " ^ " on the symbol σ_w means the estimate of σ_w.

Accordingly the distribution of the $\bar{x}$ points is affected not only by between-subgroup variation but also by within-subgroup variation. The variation of perfectly controlled state of a process is as follows.
a) The process average is constant and between-subgroup variation $\sigma_b{}^2 = 0$.
b) Variation of the process is constant, that is, within-subgroup variation $\sigma_w{}^2 = $ constant.

The between-subgroup variation cannot be obtained directly but is calculated from

$$\hat{\sigma}_b = \sqrt{\hat{\sigma}_{\bar{x}}{}^2 - \hat{\sigma}_w{}^2/n}, \tag{7.3}$$

where $\hat{\sigma}_{\bar{x}}{}^2$ is calculated from the histogram of $\bar{x}$, or from

$$\hat{\sigma}_b = \sqrt{\hat{\sigma}_x{}^2 - \hat{\sigma}_w{}^2}, \tag{7.4}$$

where $\hat{\sigma}_x{}^2$ is calculated from the histogram of x.

(3) Stratification

When the same products are made on several machines or by several operators, the data had better be classified according to machine or operator so that the difference between machines or operators can be analyzed and process control becomes easy.

Stratification is a method of identifying the source of variation of gathered data, classifying the data according to various factors.

Figure 7.5 is an example of a control chart which can be stratified. This chart shows a quality characteristic of parts manufactured by the two machines (*A* and *B*). Figure 7.6 is the stratified control chart for *A* and *B*. As a result of stratification it is found that there is almost no difference in variation between *A* and *B*, but *B* has a

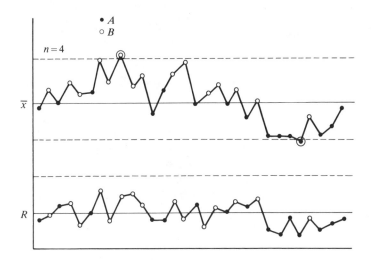

Figure 7.5   Control Chart for *A* and *B*

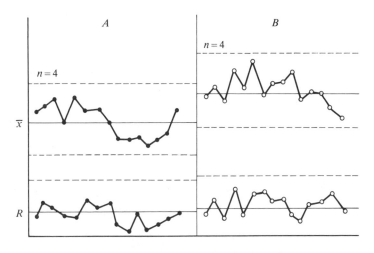

Figure 7.6   Stratified Control Charts for *A* and *B*

higher process average value than A and that the process is in the controlled state for both machines, and it can be said that between A and B, there seem some assignable causes.

Generally speaking, the purpose of stratification is to examine the difference in average values and variation between different classes and to take measures against the difference, if any. If it is impossible to take measures instantly, it is necessary to carry out process control using stratified control charts.

(4) Test of the Difference Between Stratified Control Charts

If the two stratified $\bar{x}$-R charts satisfy the following four conditions, then the difference of the average values can be tested:
a) Both charts show the controlled state.
b) The size of the subgroups is equal.
c) The values of $\bar{R}_A$ and $\bar{R}_B$ are almost equal.
d) The numbers of the subgroups k_A and k_B are large enough ($k_A > 10$, $k_B > 10$).

$$\left| \bar{x}_A - \bar{x}_B \right| \geq A_2 \bar{R} \sqrt{1/k_A + 1/k_B} , \tag{7.5}$$

where

$$\bar{R} = (k_A \bar{R}_A + k_B \bar{R}_B)/(k_A + k_B) . \tag{7.6}$$

(5) Test of the Difference in the Variation Between Strata

In order to test whether there is a difference in variation between strata after stratification, the formula (7.7) or (7.8) is used. If the formula holds, then it may be said there is a difference in the variation between A and B.

In case of $\bar{R}_A > \bar{R}_B$

$$\bar{R}_A / \bar{\bar{R}} \geq 1.2 \qquad \bar{\bar{R}} / \bar{R}_B \geq 1.2 \tag{7.7}$$

In case of $\bar{R}_B > \bar{R}_A$

$$\bar{R}_B / \bar{\bar{R}} \geq 1.2 \qquad \bar{\bar{R}} / \bar{R}_A \geq 1.2 \tag{7.8}$$

The tests mentioned in (7.5) and (7.7) or (7.8) are not necessary when the difference is obvious from the control chart at a glance.

7.6 Case Study of Process Analysis

When a control chart is used to analyze a problem, it is usually not used alone but together with histograms. Here we give an example of how to analyze a problem by the following way.

Example 7.2
In a factory manufacturing leaf springs for tractors, cracks were found in some of the springs. It is necessary to identify the cause of the trouble as quickly as possible and to prevent it from occurring again. Let us use the data given below to construct histograms and control charts in order to analyze the problem.

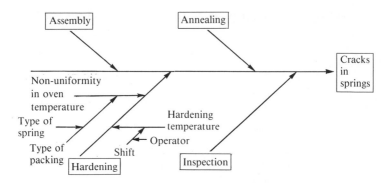

Figure 7.7   Cause-and-Effect Diagram of Cracks in Spring

Information obtained so far:
1) To identify the cause of the cracks, the above cause-and-effect diagram was drawn up.
2) Springs for small (A_1) and medium-sized (A_2) tractors are treated in the same oven. The two types of product differ only in shape, the material from which they are made being the same. However the type of packing used during heat treatment is different.
3) The demand for small tractors has increased recently, and production is gradually being stepped up. The number of springs being heat-treated at one time is being increased proportionately.
4) The oven is operated in two daily shifts (B_1 and B_2). Two heat treatments are carried out per shift, i.e., two batches of springs are heat-treated in each shift.
5) The hardness of the springs can be regarded as a substitutional characteristic for the crack.
6) The following data has been collected over the past 16 days:
   a) It was considered that the variation in the temperature of the oven from the center to the walls might be significant. Therefore after each heat treatment, one sample (P_1) was taken from the center of the oven and another (P_2) from near the wall, and their hardnesses were measured.
   b) All the springs were inspected after heat treatment, and the hardness of those with cracks was measured.
   c) The hardness standards are as follows: maximum hardness 460 Hb, minimum hardness 350 Hb.

Table 7.10 Measurements of Hardness

Day	Type of Spring A	Shift B	Lot No.	Position P_1	Position P_2	Hardness of Springs With Cracks
1	A_1	B_1	1	396	420	
			2	396	421	
		B_2	3	408	423	460
			4	408	438	
2	A_1	B_1	5	393	400	
			6	401	399	
		B_2	7	404	438	
			8	396	429	450
3	A_1	B_1	9	385	410	451
			10	391	432	456 453
		B_2	11	377	407	
			12	378	410	
4	A_1	B_1	13	387	421	456 443
			14	397	422	
		B_2	15	397	397	
			16	384	404	462 446 455
5	A_2	B_1	17	402	391	
			18	398	401	
		B_2	19	393	382	
			20	381	366	
6	A_2	B_1	21	392	411	
			22	382	399	
		B_2	23	395	402	
			24	407	381	
7	A_2	B_1	25	413	392	
			26	387	392	
		B_2	27	394	409	
			28	401	409	
8	A_2	B_1	29	401	404	
			30	400	404	
		B_2	31	414	418	
			32	406	407	

Day	Type of Spring A	Shift B	Lot No.	Position P_1	Position P_2	Hardness of Springs With Cracks
9	A_1	B_1	33	406	418	453 457
			34	397	421	
		B_2	35	436	419	
			36	400	454*	454* 449
10	A_1	B_1	37	390	432	
			38	387	422	450
		B_2	39	398	409	
			40	378	419	
11	A_1	B_1	41	390	420	
			42	417	430	445 458 473 446
		B_2	43	373	419	457 455 465
			44	385	395	458
12	A_1	B_1	45	394	406	460 455
			46	391	410	
		B_2	47	385	413	
			48	378	419	447 444 457
13	A_2	B_1	49	411	403	
			50	410	392	
		B_2	51	385	370	
			52	398	393	
14	A_2	B_1	53	394	395	
			54	397	419	
		B_2	55	409	406	
			56	397	404	
15	A_2	B_1	57	406	399	
			58	411	415	
		B_2	59	385	386	
			60	408	418	
16	A_2	B_1	61	387	410	
			62	395	401	
		B_2	63	410	395	
			64	400	409	

* The two asterisks indicate the same spring, since cracks were found in sample P_2.

Information obtained from histograms:
1) Overall histogram (Figure 7.8)
This shows approximately a normal distribution and all the samples lie within the specified hardness range. However, cracks were found in some samples of high hardness even though they were within the specification limits.

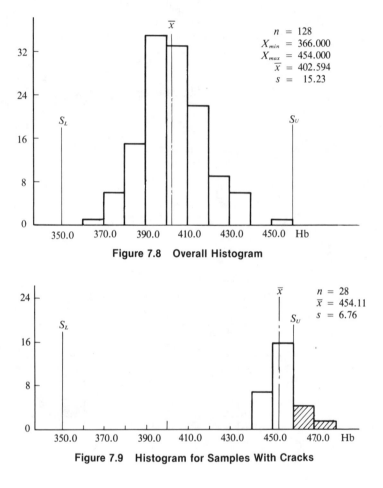

Figure 7.8   Overall Histogram

Figure 7.9   Histogram for Samples With Cracks

2) Histogram of samples with cracks (Figure 7.9)
a) All the cracked samples are of type A_1. Thus the problem lies in the treatment of type A_1 springs for small tractors.
b) The hardnesses of springs with cracks are distributed around a high value and are all higher than 440 Hb.

3) Histograms for different types of spring A_1 and A_2 (Figure 7.10)
a) The mean hardness of the springs for small tractors (A_1) is rather higher, and the individual values are more widely distributed.
b) Since all the cracked springs are type A_1 samples, the production method for springs for small tractors seems not to be adequate.
c) The distribution of the hardness values for type A_2 springs for medium-sized tractors is not wide, and there are no cracked samples among them.

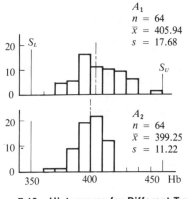

Figure 7.10   Histograms for Different Types of Srping A_1 and A_2

4) Histograms for different shifts B_1 and B_2 (Figure 7.11)

a) The mean for B_1 is higher than that for B_2, and the variation is smaller.
b) There are some springs with cracks among the B_2 samples.

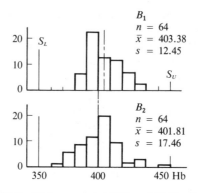

Figure 7.11   Histograms for Different Shifts B_1 and B_2

5) Histograms for different heat-treatment positions P_1 and P_2 (Figure 7.12)

a) The mean hardness of samples taken from the center of the oven (P_1) is low, and the variation is small. None of these samples has cracks.

b) The mean hardness of samples taken from near the wall of the oven (P_2) is high and the variation is slightly larger. Some of these samples contain cracks.

c) It appears that those springs treated near the wall of the oven are likely to have a high enough hardness to induce cracking.

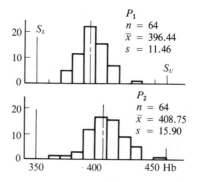

Figure 7.12   Histograms for Different Positions P_1 and P_2

6) **Histograms for different combinations of factors *A* and *B* (Figure 7.13)**

a) The variation for the combinations A_1B_1 and A_1B_2 is larger than that for either A_2B_1 or A_2B_2.

b) There is no significant difference in the means, but those for A_1B_1 and A_1B_2 are a little higher.

c) The values for the combination A_2B_1 concentrate about the mean of the specified hardness, and variation is small. Based on the present maximum and minimum hardnesses, the process capability index C_P has an extremely good value of 2.04, as calculated by

$$C_P = \frac{S_U - S_L}{6s} = \frac{460 - 350}{6 \times 8.97} = 2.04 \,.$$

Thus the combination of A_2B_1 is an excellent one.

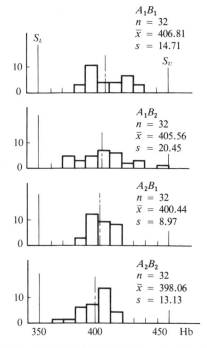

Figure 7.13 Histograms for Different Combinations of Two Factors *A* and *B*

7) **Histograms for different combinations of factors A, B and P (Figure 7.14)**

   a) The mean hardness for type A_1 samples (for small tractors) is clearly higher for samples taken from position P_2 (near the wall of the oven) than for samples taken from position P_1 (the center of the oven).
   b) The mean hardness for type A_2 samples (for medium-sized tractors) does not appear to depend on the position from which the samples are taken.
   c) The standard deviation has the same value of about 10 Hb for the combinations $(A_1B_1P_1)$, $(A_1B_1P_2)$, $(A_2B_1P_1)$, $(A_2B_1P_2)$ and $(A_2B_2P_1)$. It has a larger vaue of about 15 Hb for the combinations $(A_1B_2P_1)$, $(A_1B_2P_2)$ and $(A_2B_2P_2)$. This difference appears to be due to factor B, with B_2 giving a larger variation.
   d) Combinations $(A_2B_1P_1)$, $(A_2B_1P_2)$ and $(A_2B_2P_1)$ concentrate about the mean of the specified hardness and variation is small.

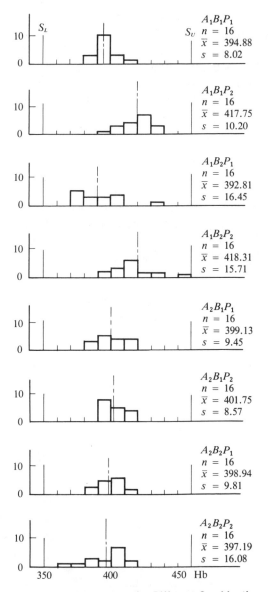

$A_1B_1P_1$
$n = 16$
$\bar{x} = 394.88$
$s = 8.02$

$A_1B_1P_2$
$n = 16$
$\bar{x} = 417.75$
$s = 10.20$

$A_1B_2P_1$
$n = 16$
$\bar{x} = 392.81$
$s = 16.45$

$A_1B_2P_2$
$n = 16$
$\bar{x} = 418.31$
$s = 15.71$

$A_2B_1P_1$
$n = 16$
$\bar{x} = 399.13$
$s = 9.45$

$A_2B_1P_2$
$n = 16$
$\bar{x} = 401.75$
$s = 8.57$

$A_2B_2P_1$
$n = 16$
$\bar{x} = 398.94$
$s = 9.81$

$A_2B_2P_2$
$n = 16$
$\bar{x} = 397.19$
$s = 16.08$

Figure 7.14   Histograms for Different Combinations
of Three Factors *A, B* and *P*

Information obtained from $\bar{x}$-R *chart* **(Figure 7.15):**

1) Overall control chart

Since the data is subgrouped according to lots, the variation within a subgroup is the variation within a lot, i.e., the variation between P_1 and P_2, the sampling error and the measurement error. The variation between different subgroups includes the variation between lots and those between shifts, different types of spring, and different days (Table 7.11).

  a) R chart

    i) None of the values lies outside the control limits, but the long series of relatively smoothly-connected values for lots 7—14, 26—33 and 51—64 are abnormal, and indicate that the process is in an out-of-control state.

    ii) R is relatively large for the type A_1 (small tractor) springs and relatively small for the type A_2 (medium-sized tractor) springs. These two types should therefore be classified separately.

  b) $\bar{x}$ chart

    No points lie outside the control limits, but the long series of values for lots 15—26, 31—39 and 43—53 are abnormal, indicating an out-of-control state.

Table 7.11 Subgroups of Overall Control Chart

Day	Type of Spring	Shift	Lot No.	Position	
	A	B		P_1	P_2
1	A_1	B_1	1	396	420
			2	396	421
		B_2	3	408	423
			4	408	438
2	A_1	B_1	5	393	400
			6	401	399
		B_2	7	404	438
			8	396	429
3	A_1	B_1	9	385	410
			10	391	432
		B_2	11	377	407
			12	378	410

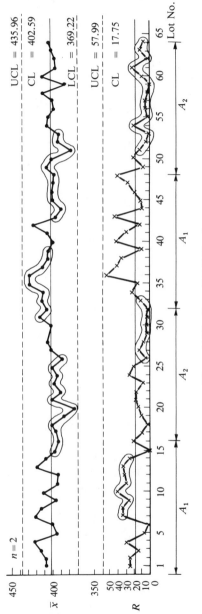

Figure 7.15 Overall $\bar{x}$-R Chart

2) Control charts stratified according to factors A and B (Figure 7.16)

Since the data is subgrouped by lot, the variation within a subgroup is the same as the variation within the corresponding lot. The variation between subgroups includes the variation between lots and the daily variation (Table 7.12).

Table 7.12 Subgroups of Control Charts Stratified According to Two Factors A and B

Day	Type of Spring	Shift	Lot No.	Position	
	A	B		P_1	P_2
1	A_1	B_1	1	396	420
			2	396	421
		B_2	3	408	423
			4	408	438
2	A_1	B_1	5	393	400
			6	401	399
		B_2	7	404	438
			8	396	429
3	A_1	B_1	9	385	410
			10	391	432
		B_2	11	377	407
			12	378	410

a) (A_1B_1): The R chart and the $\bar{x}$ chart both exhibit an approach to the central line. Each subgroup is composed of data on springs taken both from the center of the oven and from near the wall. This tendency is therefore the result of the different means of these two distributions. It is necessary to stratify the data according to position (P).

b) (A_1B_2): The same can be said as about the charts for (A_1B_1).

c) (A_2B_1): Both the R and the $\bar{x}$ charts are in the controlled state. In other words, there is no variation between subgroups (i.e., between lots and from day to day). The process is in stable operation. Let us estimate the standard deviation within a lot, σ_w.

In this case
$$n = 2, d_2 = 1.128,$$
so we have
$$\hat{\sigma}_w = \bar{R}/d_2 = 10.75/1.128 = 9.53$$
This is approximately the same as the value of $\hat{\sigma}_x$, where $\hat{\sigma}_x = s = 8.97$, estimated from the histogram of Figure 7.13 (A_2B_1).

d) (A_2B_2): The R chart is in the controlled state. However, the $\bar{x}$ chart includes three points lying outside the control limits, and is not in the controlled state. There is a variation between subgroups; that is, between different lots and different days. The production method used in shift B_2 should be examined. The estimated variation within lots, σ_w, is

$$\hat{\sigma}_w = \bar{R}/d_2 = 8.42.$$

The standard deviation obtained from Figure 7.13 (A_2B_2) is 13.13. Since σ_x^2 is expressed by

$$\sigma_x^2 = \sigma_w^2 + \sigma_b^2 ,$$

the variation between lots $\hat{\sigma}_b$ is given by

$$\hat{\sigma}_b = \sqrt{\hat{\sigma}_x^2 - \hat{\sigma}_w^2} = \sqrt{13.13^2 - 8.42^2} = 10.07 .$$

In other words, the variation between subgroups is of the same order as the variation within subgroups.

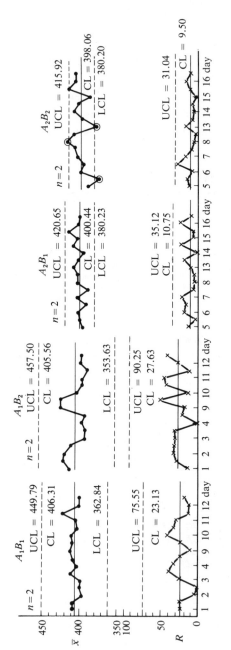

Figure 7.16 $\bar{x}$-R Charts Stratified According to Two Factors A and B

3) Control charts for type A_1 springs stratified according to B and P (Figure 7.17)

Since the mean differs depending on the position in the oven, control charts were made according to position (P), combining the data for two lots each day into one subgroup. Thus the variation within a subgroup consists of the variation during a single day, which includes the variation between lots. The variation between subgroups consists of the variation between days (Table 7.13).

Table 7.13 Subgrouping of Control Charts for Type A_1 Springs Stratified According to B and P

Day	Type of Spring	Shift	Lot No.	Position	
	A	B		P_1	P_2
1	A_1	B_1	1	396	420
			2	396	421
		B_2	3	408	423
			4	408	438
2	A_1	B_1	5	393	400
			6	401	399
		B_2	7	404	438
			8	396	429
3	A_1	B_1	9	385	410
			10	391	432
		B_2	11	377	407
			12	378	410

a) The difference in $\bar{x}$ for $(A_1B_1P_1)$ and $(A_1B_1P_2)$ is obvious. One point lies outside the control limits, but both the $\bar{x}$ and the R charts show a relatively stable control state.

b) A comparison of P_1 and P_2 for the combination A_1B_1.
Since $\bar{R}$ is approximately the same for $(A_1B_1P_1)$ and $(A_1B_1P_2)$, the data for these can be pooled to estimate σ_w, then

$$\hat{\sigma}_w = \bar{R}/d_2 = \frac{8.25 + 6.50}{2 \times 1.128} = 6.54.$$

As for σ_b, which includes the difference depending on the position, it is obtained by

$$\hat{\sigma}_b = \sqrt{\hat{\sigma}_x{}^2 - \hat{\sigma}_w{}^2} = \sqrt{14.71^2 - 6.54^2} = 13.18 .$$

The contribution of the between-subgroup variation to the overall variation $\sigma_x{}^2$ can be expressed as the percentage $\hat{\rho}_b$.

$$\hat{\rho}_b = \hat{\sigma}_b{}^2 / \hat{\sigma}_x{}^2 \times 100 = (13.18^2 / 14.71^2) \times 100 = 80\% .$$

In this case, $\hat{\sigma}_b{}^2$ depends on the position in the oven, also indicating that the hardness of the springs is biased according to their position in the oven, and that this should be improved.

c) If we compare Figure 7.16 (A_1B_1) with Figure 7.17 $(A_1B_1P_1)$, we see that, in the latter chart, stratifying the former by P has resulted in a stably-controlled state. This is because the composition of the subgroups has changed. The data should be grouped so as to make within-subgroup variation as random as possible, making the variation due to the process appear in between-subgroup variation.

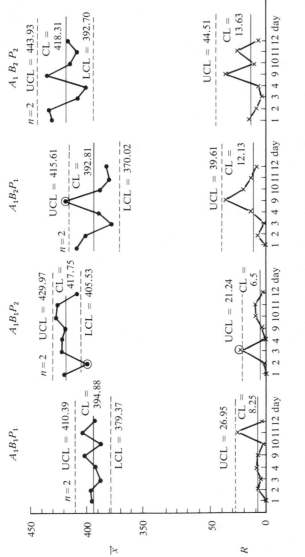

Figure 7.17 $\bar{x}$-R Charts for Type A_1 Springs Stratified According to B and P

4) Control charts for type A_2 springs stratified according to B (Figure 7.18)

With regard to type A_2, there is no difference in hardness depending on the position in the oven, and the data was grouped in two lots each day with $n = 4$. Thus the within-subgroup variation is composed of the daily variation including the variation both within and between lots. The variation between subgroups is the variation between days.

a) (A_2B_1): The $\bar{x}$ and the R charts are both in the controlled state. σ_w is estimated from

$$\hat{\sigma}_w = \bar{R}/d_2 = 19.13/2.059 = 9.29 ,$$

b) (A_2B_2): The R chart is in the controlled state, but the $\bar{x}$ chart is not. A point is outside the control limits, and an approach to the control limits is observed.

Table 7.14   Subgrouping of Control Charts for Type A_2 Springs Stratified According to B

Day	Type of Spring A	Shift B	Lot No.	Position	
				P_1	P_2
4	A_1	B_1	13	387	421
			14	397	422
		B_2	15	397	397
			16	384	404
5	A_2	B_1	17	402	391
			18	398	401
		B_2	19	393	382
			20	381	366
6	A_2	B_1	21	392	411
			22	382	399
		B_2	23	395	402
			24	407	381

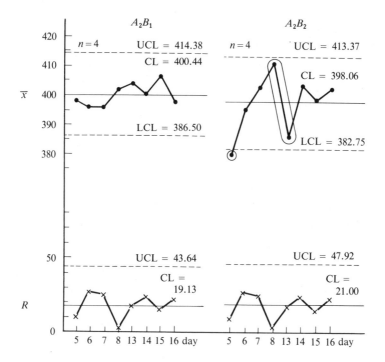

Figure 7.18 Control Charts for Type A_2 Springs Stratified According to B

Summary and countermeasures:

1) Cracks have appeared in the springs for small tractors. It is thought that this is due to the method by which the springs for small tractors are packed in the heat treatment oven. When the small springs are heat-treated, a difference in temperature is produced at the center of the oven in comparison with the position near the wall. This is thought to increase the hardness of the springs and give rise to cracking. It is therefore necessary to change the method of packing to the one which causes a temperature difference no greater than that which is at present produced when medium-sized springs are treated.

2) There is a problem with the setting of the operation standards. It is necessary to establish the relation between the hardness of the springs and their propensity to crack, and set new standards. As a temporary estimate based on the data given here, the maximum

hardness should be set at 440Hb below which there are no cracks found. If the hardness is controlled below 440Hb, cracking may not occur.

3) A comparison of different shifts showed that operation in shift B_2 was not stable. The operation standards and methods should be reviewed. The reason why there is no variation between lots in a day but there is variation from day to day should be investigated.

4) If the above actions are taken, the process capability presently obtained with the combination A_2B_1 can be expected to be obtained for both small and medium-sized springs, and defects will be eliminated and the process capability index will be

$$C_P = \frac{S_U - S_L}{6s} = \frac{440 - 350}{6 \times 8.97} = 1.67 .$$

7.7 Process Control by Control Charts

When the relation between a quality characteristic and the affecting process factors has been grasped sufficiently, next step is to control these factors at certain levels so that the target value of quality characteristic is kept in a desirable range. This step is called process control. The control chart serves as a helpful means to identify abnormal conditions of processes and to maintain processes at a stable condition.

(1) Control Characteristics

A variable which is used to conduct control of a process is called the control characteristic of the process. The following considerations should be given in the determination of control characteristics.

a) Characteristic values should correctly reflect the states of process.

b) Effects from outside areas should be minimized.

c) Results should be immediately available.

d) Sampling and measurement should be economical.

A substitutional characteristic can be used if this characterstic has strong relation to the original control characteristic. In the case of materials that need to be destroyed for measurement, non-destructive measurement may substitute.

(2) Determination of the Control Lines

For managing a process by the use of a control chart, it is necessary to examine adequacy of process capability; that is to say, whether the process is stable and whether the ranges of the variation of a control characteristic in a chart indicate satisfactory conformance to the standard needed to produce a certain product. When the process is found to be inadequate and its control characteristic is not in a controlled state, it is necessary to start tentative control activities against abnormalities by setting temporary control lines, and improve the process at the same time.

The control chart which is made for process analysis is checked against standard values. If the control chart shows that the process is in a desirable state, then control lines are extended for the control of the process. Its procedure is given in Figure 7.19.

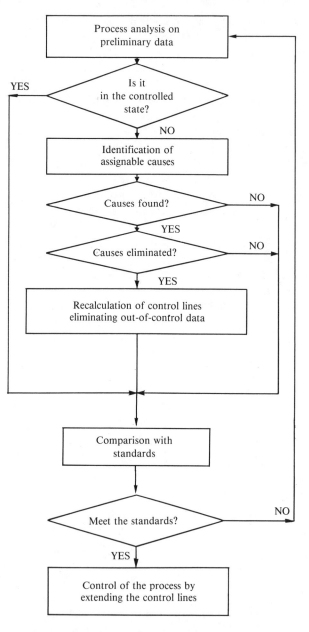

Figure 7.19 Flow of Decisions of Control Lines

(3) Revision of the Control Lines

Control lines need to be revised when technical changes in the state of process is recognized. This revision should be done as quickly as possible. Even when no conspicuous changes are recognized, regular check-ups of control lines should be maintained. Its revision should be based on the range of fluctuations that may occur when the process is well-controlled.

(4) Operation Standards

In order to put an entire process in a stable state through process control, it is necessary to grasp the contributing factors to process's fluctuations and to avoid abnormal changes of these factors. Standardization of operation procedures and methods is needed to achieve this. In drafting a set of operation standards, the following considerations should be taken.

a) The standardization should be consistent with the above-mentioned objectives.
b) Standards should be so established to control the fluctuation of the contributing factors.
c) Standards should be practical and be a criterion of operation.
d) Standards are tentative decisions and not necessarily are ideal goals.
e) Standards should specify the important procedures.
f) Revisions of standards should be made for improvement.
g) The background of making standards should be clearly understood, and the process of making standards should also be made clear.
h) Standards should state responsibility and authorization clearly.
i) In documentation of standards, the usability of such manuals should be taken into account.
j) Temporary measures against emergencies should be described.
k) Considerations for fool-proof and for safety should be taken.
l) Be goal-oriented, but not be formality-oriented.
m) Instruction and training should be implemented.

In the planning of standards, the ability to control main factors of process is indispensable. Also, success of standardization depends upon workers' devotion to the standards. Standards should be continuously revised to perfection in conducting process control using the control chart. In addition, the related procedures of the standardization should also be established such as application, documentation, revision, education, and training.

(5) Comparison With Specifications

When the comparison of process data with specification limits is to be made, this should be done with the unit specified in the specification. If the specification limits are applied to each individual item, specification limits should be compared with the data of each item, not with $\bar{x}$ or control limits.

If the histogram lies within the upper limit and the lower limit of specification with margin, it can be judged to be satisfactory for the standards. This process can be controlled by the control lines calculated by the process data.

On the other hand, if the histogram goes beyond upper and lower limits, it means a process is not satisfactory. Remedial procedures are necessary.

Even though a process is in the controlled state, nonconforming products could be produced from the process, and vice versa. Control limits are made to provide judgement on whether the process is in the controlled state or not, while specification limits are made to provide judgement on whether each product is defective or not. The controlled state is a state in which assignable causes are removed and the process variation is only due to chance causes. It can be obtained by operating the job according to the work instructions. The width of control limits is determined based on variation due to chance causes. On the other hand, specification limits are decided by demands of consumers or users.

Thus, as shown in Figure 7.20, you are likely to have following four cases:
a) Process is not in the controlled state and also defectives are produced.
b) Process is in the controlled state yet defectives are produced.
c) Process is not in the controlled state but products are nondefectives.

d) Process is in the controlled state and also products are non-defectives.

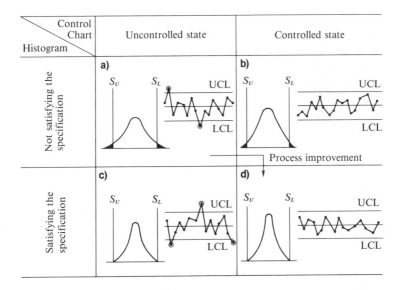

Figure 7.20   Comparison of Control Charts With Specifications

There are no problems in the case of d), but it is confusing when b) or c) occurs. The reason is a disharmony of process capability and specification. In the case of b), the process capability is insufficient for the specification. For preventing the occurrence of the defectives, the effort to improve the process capability should be done. Case c) occurs when the process has sufficient capability for the specification. In this case, improvement on the production efficiency should be considered.

Exercise 7.1
Select an appropriate type of control chart in order to control the following control characteristics.
1) Weight of packed cookies.
2) The number of defectives in 1000 parts.
3) The number of soldering defects in a radio set.
4) Yield of a chemical product in a batch.
5) Percent defective of a lot, the size of which might vary.

6) The strength of five test pieces sampled in a day.
7) The number of scratches per 1m² in a steel plate.

Exercise 7.2

To investigate the manner of variation in a machining process of certain parts, dimensions of the parts were measured four times a day, at 9:00, 11:00, 14:00 and 16:00, as shown below. Make an $\bar{x}$-R chart to analyze this process.

No.	Date	Time			
		9:00	11:00	14:00	16:00
1	Nov. 2	52.5	52.9	52.9	53.5
2	3	53.0	52.8	53.5	52.4
3	4	52.8	52.9	52.7	52.8
4	5	52.9	52.9	52.9	52.9
5	6	52.8	52.9	52.7	53.1
6	9	52.6	53.4	53.1	53.3
7	10	53.5	53.6	52.8	52.7
8	11	53.1	53.3	53.5	53.0
9	12	53.4	53.1	53.1	53.1
10	13	53.2	53.4	53.1	52.9
11	16	53.4	53.0	53.9	53.1
12	17	52.8	52.9	53.2	53.2
13	18	53.2	53.3	52.9	53.1
14	19	53.5	52.9	54.0	53.9
15	20	54.3	53.6	53.6	53.8
16	23	53.2	53.3	54.0	53.7
17	24	53.8	54.0	53.8	53.8
18	25	53.1	53.6	53.7	53.8
29	26	53.7	53.8	53.0	53.5
30	27	53.3	53.1	53.6	53.0
21	30	53.3	53.7	53.3	53.8
22	Dec. 1	53.1	53.1	53.2	53.1
23	2	53.6	53.4	53.2	53.0
24	3	53.4	53.7	53.0	53.2
25	4	53.3	53.2	53.5	53.4

Exercise 7.3

Correct errors, if any, in the following sentences.
1) In an $\bar{x}$-R chart, $\bar{x}$ chart shows a change in a subgroup mean and R chart shows a change in the variation within a subgroup.
2) In an $\bar{x}$-R chart, we check whether there is between-subgroup variation on the basis of within-subgroup variation.

3) When all the points plotted in a control chart are between control limits, we consider the process is in the controlled state.

4) In an $\bar{x}$-R chart, a point will fall outside the limits, even if there is no change in the process.

5) In a control chart where small value of control characteristic is desirable, the LCL is of no use in practice.

6) When a control chart shows the controlled state, the process will produce products conforming to the specification.

7) Suppose a point falls outside the control limits. If the specification limits are wide, we have only to take care of the process. But if the specification limits are narrow, we should promptly find out the cause and take an appropriate action.

8) When an $\bar{x}$-R chart shows the statistically controlled state, we can grasp the process capability by a histogram of x (raw data).

9) In an $\bar{x}$ chart, successive fifteen points are between control limits $\pm$ 1-sigma, the process is in a perfect stable state. We should try to keep this state.

Chapter **8**

Additivity of Variances

8.1 The Means and the Variances of Sums

Before throwing a die, we do not know which face will be up, but if it is an unloaded die, the probability of each face appearing at the top is 1/6. The expected value of the number of dots is

$$\mu = 1 \times \frac{1}{6} + 2 \times \frac{1}{6} + \cdots + 6 \times \frac{1}{6} = 3.5 .$$

The variance of the number of dots is

$$\sigma^2 = \sum_{x=1}^{6} (x - 3.5)^2 \times \frac{1}{6} = \frac{35}{12} , \qquad (8.1)$$

and their standard deviation is

$$\sigma = \sqrt{\frac{35}{12}} = 1.71. \qquad (8.2)$$

When a die is thrown twice and the sum of the numbers of dots is obtained, it will be some value from 2 to 12, and their relative frequencies can be obtained from Table 8.1. In this case, the values appear at different frequencies, 7 being the most frequent and 2 and 12 the least frequent. What are the mean and the variance of the sums of the numbers of dots in this case?

First, the mean is

$$\mu = \Sigma x P(x)$$

$$= 2 \times \frac{1}{36} + 3 \times \frac{2}{36} + \cdots + 6 \times \frac{5}{36} + 7 \times \frac{6}{36}$$

$$+ 8 \times \frac{5}{36} + \cdots + 12 \times \frac{1}{36} = 7. \qquad (8.3)$$

The variance is

$$\sigma^2 = \Sigma (x - \mu)^2 P(x)$$

$$= (2-7)^2 \times \frac{1}{36} + (3-7)^2 \times \frac{2}{36} + \cdots$$

$$+ (7-7)^2 \times \frac{6}{36} + \cdots + (12-7)^2 \times \frac{1}{36}$$

$$= \frac{35}{6} \ . \tag{8.4}$$

Table 8.1 Sum of the Number of Dots Obtained From Two Throws of the Die

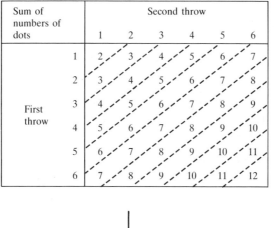

Sum of numbers of dots		Second throw					
		1	2	3	4	5	6
First throw	1	2	3	4	5	6	7
	2	3	4	5	6	7	8
	3	4	5	6	7	8	9
	4	5	6	7	8	9	10
	5	6	7	8	9	10	11
	6	7	8	9	10	11	12

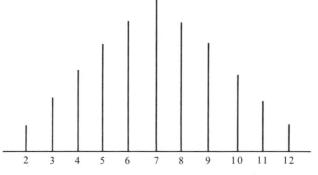

Figure 8.1 Relative Frequencies of the Sum of the Number of Dots Obtained When the Die Is Thrown Twice

From this, we learn that the mean and the variance of the sums of the numbers of dots obtained for two throws of a die are both twice those values obtained for one throw.

Next, let us do the same for the difference in the number of dots. That is, what will be the difference value when the second value is subtracted from the first? As we can see from Table 8.2, the data consists of values from -5 to $+5$, and as far as the relative frequency is concerned, 0 is the most frequent, and the relative frequencies of each value are as in Figure 8.2, which is the same as Figure 8.1 except that the numbers have been shifted by seven to the left. From this we learn that the mean and the variance of the differences are

$$\mu = 0,$$ (8.5)

and

$$\sigma^2 = \frac{35}{6}.$$ (8.6)

Note that the variances of the sums and differences are the same.

Table 8.2   Difference Between First Throw and Second Throw

Difference between first throw and second throw	Second throw					
	1	2	3	4	5	6
First throw 1	0	−1	−2	−3	−4	−5
2	1	0	−1	−2	−3	−4
3	2	1	0	−1	−2	−3
4	3	2	1	0	−1	−2
5	4	3	2	1	0	−1
6	5	4	3	2	1	0

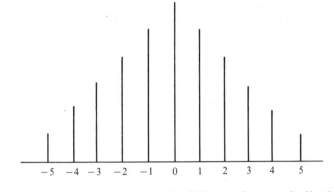

Figure 8.2   Relative Frequencies of the Difference Between the Number of Dots Obtained After the First and Second Throws of the Die

8.2 Precision of Parts Assembly

Suppose that we have a product which, as Figure 8.3-a shows, is made by joining parts A and B together. When the dimension x of part A has a distribution of mean μ_x and standard deviation σ_x, and the dimension y of part B has a distribution of mean μ_y and standard deviation σ_y, then the mean and the variance of the dimension z when samples of the two parts are randomly selected and joined are:

$$\mu_z = \mu_x + \mu_y, \tag{8.7}$$

and

$$\sigma_z^{\,2} = \sigma_x^{\,2} + \sigma_y^{\,2}. \tag{8.8}$$

When two parts are randomly selected and joined together as in Figure 8.3-b, we have

$$\mu_z = \mu_x - \mu_y, \tag{8.9}$$

and

$$\sigma_z^{\,2} = \sigma_x^{\,2} + \sigma_y^{\,2} \tag{8.10}$$

for the dimension z. The mean of z is given by the difference between the means of A and B. But the variance of z is the sum of the variances of the two.

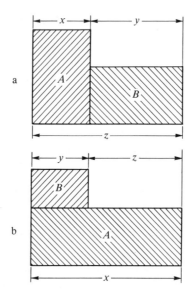

Figure 8.3   Parts Assembly

8.3 Theoretical Formulas

When z is defined by

$$z = ax + by \tag{8.11}$$

where a and b are constant coefficients, the mean of z is given by

$$\mu_z = a\mu_x + b\mu_y , \tag{8.12}$$

where μ_x, and μ_y are the means of x and y. If x and y are independent, the variance of z is given by

$$\sigma_z^2 = a^2\sigma_x^2 + b^2\sigma_y^2 , \tag{8.13}$$

where σ_x^2 and σ_y^2 are the variances of x and y.

In the assembled parts described in the previous section, $a = 1$ and $b = \pm 1$. Since the squares of coefficients are added, the variance becomes a sum even when the particular case involves a difference of random variables. This characteristic is called the *additivity of variances*.

Generally, if $x_1, x_2, \cdots, x_n$ are independent random variables and their mean values and variances are $\mu_1, \cdots, \mu_n$, and $\sigma_1^2, \cdots, \sigma_n^2$, respectively, the expectation and the variance of

$$y = a_1 x_1 + a_2 x_2 + \cdots + a_n x_n \qquad (8.14)$$

are given by

$$\mu_y = a_1 \mu_1 + \cdots + a_n \mu_n , \qquad (8.15)$$

and

$$\sigma_y^2 = a_1^2 \sigma_1^2 + \cdots + a_n^2 \sigma_n^2 . \qquad (8.16)$$

8.4 The Expectation and the Variance Of Sample Means

When n measurements are taken from a population with population mean μ and population variance σ^2, and the values of the measurements are $x_1, x_2, \cdots, x_n$ and their mean is y, then

$$y = \frac{1}{n} \sum_{i=1}^{n} x_i = \frac{1}{n} x_1 + \frac{1}{n} x_2 + \cdots + \frac{1}{n} x_n . \qquad (8.17)$$

From the above formula, putting $a_1 = a_2 = \ldots = a_n = 1/n$, the expectation and the variance of y are obtained by

$$\mu_y = \mu , \qquad (8.18)$$

and

$$\sigma_y^2 = \left(\frac{1}{n}\right)^2 n \sigma^2 = \frac{\sigma^2}{n} . \qquad (8.19)$$

This is a well known formula for the distribution of the sample mean.

8.5 Sampling Error and Measurement Error

When estimating an ingredient of such materials as coal and iron ore, generally the work is done in two stages, the first of which is taking a sample from the lot, and the second stage is the chemical analysis of the obtained sample. Because of these procedures, two kinds of error exist in the estimation of the ingredient. One is called the sampling error and it occurs when the sample is taken from the lot, and the other is called the measurement error which occurs when the sample is measured. When the sampling error is expressed as x_S and the measurement error as x_M, the measured data y can be expressed as

$$y = \mu + x_S + x_M , \tag{8.20}$$

where μ is the true value of the lot. If the mean of x_S is μ_S and that of x_M is μ_M, the mean of y is given by

$$\mu_y = \mu + \mu_S + \mu_M , \tag{8.21}$$

where μ_S and μ_M are the bias in sampling and measurement, respectively. The variance of y is given by

$$\sigma_y^2 = \sigma_S^2 + \sigma_M^2 , \tag{8.22}$$

where σ_S^2 is the sampling precision and σ_M^2 is the measurement precision.

When one sample is measured twice and the mean is taken, the variance of the mean is

$$\sigma_{\bar{y}}^2 = \sigma_S^2 + \frac{\sigma_M^2}{2} . \tag{8.23}$$

The variance of the measurement error becomes a half. If we take two samples, make measurements on each of them once and get their mean, then its variance is given by

$$\sigma_{\bar{y}}^2 = \frac{\sigma_S^2}{2} + \frac{\sigma_M^2}{2} , \tag{8.24}$$

and in this case the variance of the sampling error also becomes a half.

As explained in the previous section, the variance of the mean value becomes $1/n$, if the measurements are repeated n times, but if errors are involved in several stages as in this example, the components of the variance are reduced in different ways depending on what stage the repetition is made.

Errors can be classified into two categories, bias and variation. While variation is reduced when measurements are repeated, bias remains the same no matter how many observations are repeated, and obtaining the mean does not lead to its reduction.

8.6 The Variance of Function Values

When y is expressed by a function f of independent random variables $x_1, x_2, \cdots, x_n$, as

$$y = f(x_1, x_2, \cdots, x_n), \tag{8.25}$$

and f is expanded around $\mu_1, \cdots, \mu_n$, which are mean values of $x_1, \cdots, x_n$, then

$$
\begin{aligned}
y &= f(x_1, \cdots, x_n) \\
&= f(\mu_1, \cdots, \mu_n) + \sum_{i=1}^{n} \left(\frac{\partial f}{\partial x_i} \right)(x_i - \mu_i) \\
&\quad + \sum_{i=1}^{n}\sum_{j=1}^{n} \frac{\partial^2 f}{\partial x_i \partial x_j}(x_i - \mu_i)(x_j - \mu_j) + \cdots
\end{aligned}
\tag{8.26}
$$

If the terms of the second and higher degrees can be ignored, it is possible to write

$$
\begin{aligned}
y &\doteqdot f(\mu_1, \cdots, \mu_n) \\
&\quad + \sum_{i=1}^{n} \frac{\partial f}{\partial x_i}(x_i - \mu_i)
\end{aligned}
\tag{8.27}
$$

and consequently the mean and the variance of y are approximately

$$\mu_y \doteqdot f(\mu_1, \cdots, \mu_n) \tag{8.28}$$

and

$$\sigma_y^2 \doteq \sum_{i=1}^{n} \left(\frac{\partial f}{\partial x_i} \right)^2 \sigma_i^2 , \tag{8.29}$$

where σ_i^2 is the variance of x_i.

Example 8.1   Weight of Dry Coal
About 1,000 tons of coal were delivered. Its average moisture content is about 8%. If the precision of weighing the coal, σ_1, is 5 tons and the precision of sampling and measurement of the moisture, σ_2, is 0.5%, what is the precision, σ_y, of y, the estimated weight of the coal when it is dry?

Let the measured weight of the coal be x_1 tons and moisture content be x_2%, then the weight of dry coal is estimated by

$$y = x_1 \left(1 - \frac{x_2}{100} \right) . \tag{8.30}$$

Consequently,

$$\sigma_y^2 \doteq \left(1 - \frac{x_2}{100} \right)^2 \sigma_1^2 + x_1^2 \left(\frac{\sigma_2}{100} \right)^2$$

$$= \left(\frac{92}{100} \right)^2 \times 5^2 + 1000^2 \left(\frac{0.5}{100} \right)^2 = 46.16 . \tag{8.31}$$

Thus

$$\sigma_y = 6.8 \text{ (tons)}. \tag{8.32}$$

8.7 When Random Variables Are Not Independent

The additivity of variances works well when the random variables are mutually independent. Two random variables are said to be independent when the value of one variable varies without any relation to the other variable.

When there are n married couples and the ages of a husband and his wife are x and y, respectively, the difference between their ages is expressed by

$$z = x - y .\tag{8.33}$$

If x and y are independent, the variance z will be

$$\sigma_z^2 = \sigma_x^2 + \sigma_y^2 .\tag{8.34}$$

Suppose $\sigma_x = \sigma_y = 5$, then $\sigma_z \doteqdot 7$. But in reality, this does not happen, because the ages of a husband and his wife are not independent. For an aged couple, both the man and his wife are old, and for a young couple, they are both young. This is not to say that there are no old men married to young women or aged women with young men, but such cases are far less than the first two cases.

When x and y are not independent, the mean and the variance of

$$z = ax + by\tag{8.35}$$

are given by

$$\mu_z = a\mu_x + b\mu_y ,\tag{8.36}$$

and

$$\sigma_z^2 = a^2\sigma_x^2 + b^2\sigma_y^2 + 2ab\rho\sigma_x\sigma_y .\tag{8.37}$$

The mean of z is the same as in the case when x and y are independent, but the variance differs by $2ab\rho\sigma_x\sigma_y$, where ρ is the correlation coefficient, a coefficient which shows the degree of relationship between two variables. The values of ρ is between -1 and $+1$, that is

$$-1 \leqq \rho \leqq 1.\tag{8.38}$$

The stronger is the relationship between the two variables, the closer is the absolute value of ρ to 1.

When $\rho = \pm 1$, all (x, y) are on a straight line. When $\rho > 0$, the increase of one tends to increase the other and is called positive correlation, and when $\rho < 0$, the increase of one tends to decrease the other and is called negative correlation. In the case of the ages of men and their wives, clearly $\rho > 0$. For example, if $\rho = 0.7$ the variance of the age differences will be

$$\sigma_z^2 = 5^2 + 5^2 - 2 \times 0.7 \times 5 \times 5 = 15 ,\tag{8.39}$$

$$\sigma_z \doteqdot 3.87 .\tag{8.40}$$

8.8 Selective Combination

When parts are randomly selected and assembled, the variances of the sums and differences of the dimensions of these parts are each the sum of the variances of each part because of the additivity of variances, as described in Section 8.2, and the variation will always be greater than that of the original parts. The orthodox way to reduce the variation of a product is to reduce the variations of its individual parts. However, if it is too difficult to do this for technological reasons of the production, it is necessary to choose the most suitable "partner" for a part rather than select them at random.

For example, the gap between an engine piston and its cylinder has a great effect on the performance of the engine. If the diameter of the cylinder is x and the diameter of the piston is y, it is necessary to keep the value of $z = x - y$ as uniform as possible. From the formula described in Section 8.7, we get

$$\sigma_z^2 = \sigma_x^2 + \sigma_y^2 - 2\rho\sigma_x\sigma_y . \tag{8.41}$$

So, if ρ is made to approach 1, σ_z^2 will come close to $(\sigma_x - \sigma_y)^2$.

A camera lens is made by laminating lenses of different refraction indices in order to reduce chromatic aberration. If the thickness of one lens is x and that of the other lens is y, it is desirable to maintain the overall thickness $z = x + y$ as uniform as possible.

Since

$$\sigma_z^2 = \sigma_x^2 + \sigma_y^2 + 2\rho\sigma_x\sigma_y,$$

σ_z^2 will approach $(\sigma_x - \sigma_y)^2$, if ρ is made to approach -1, as in the previous example.

Although selective combination is an effective way to reduce variation, it lowers production efficiency because more parts are required and each part has to be measured in advance.

8.9 Statistical Quality Control

Industrial production often involves mass production of the same type of product. It is necessary to keep the variation in the quality characteristics of these products to a minimum, and to achieve this is one of the main tasks in quality control. The variations in quality characteristics are caused by changes in a large number of factors which affect these characteristics. These can be broadly classified into the following four elements.

1) Variations in the materials.
2) Variations in machines and equipment.
3) Variations in men and methods (workers and operation methods).
4) Variations in measurements.

These are called the 4M's of variations, and variations in quality characteristics appear as the sum of these four types of variations according to the principle of the additivity of variances. We must find out how strongly these elements contribute to the variations in quality and which variations must be controlled, and devise the means to control them. The basic quality control activities at the factory are repeated analyses and improvements in order to reduce quality variations. With this as a starting point, it is necessary to determine the magnitude of the present quality fluctuations, and then to proceed with the analysis of factors which cause them.

From the theorem of additivity of variances, we can derive an important law as follows:

"Reduce larger variance in order to reduce total variance."

Table 8.3   Reducing Larger Variance to Reduce Total Variance

Case No.	σ_x	σ_y	$\sigma_z^2 = \sigma_x^2 + \sigma_y^2$	σ_z
1	10	10	200	14.1
2	10	5	125	11.2
3	10	3	109	10.4
4	10	1	101	10.05
5	5	5	50	7.07
6	5	3	34	5.83
7	5	1	26	5.10

Table 8.3 shows several cases of the values of σ_x and σ_y, and $\sigma_z^2 = \sigma_x^2 + \sigma_y^2$. From this we can see that the contribution of σ_x to σ_z is much larger than σ_y except when $\sigma_x = \sigma_y$. It means that we should reduce the larger variance σ_x^2 first when we want to reduce the total variance σ_z^2.

Exercise 8.1
Two types of parts, A and B, are picked randomly and assembled together. The following data is the measured value of each part before assembly.
1) Obtain the variances of A and B.
2) Obtain the value of $A + B$ for each set and compute the variance.
3) Do the same computation for $A - B$.

No.	A	B	No.	A	B
1	6.95	5.40	6	7.70	3.90
2	6.75	4.45	7	6.85	4.25
3	7.25	4.65	8	7.50	3.95
4	6.50	4.55	9	7.05	4.80
5	7.95	4.95	10	7.90	4.90

Exercise 8.2
There is a filling machine which stops the filling operation automatically when the sum of the weight of the container and its contents reaches a pre-set value. What is the variation of the weight of the contents when the filling precision of this machine in terms of standard deviation is σ_1 and the variation of the container weight is σ_2 in terms of standard deviation?

Chapter 9

Introduction to Statistical Inference

9.1 Statistics

When we want to estimate the mean of a population, we take a set of observations from the population and calculate the mean of the observations. A value calculated from a sample, such as the sample mean, is called a *statistic*. In other words, a statistic is a function of sample observations.

We should distinguish a statistic from a population parameter. To do this, we often use the terms *sample mean* and *population mean* instead of mean simply. A population parameter has a certain constant value, but is not actually known. On the other hand, we can calculate a statistic from a sample, but the statistic will vary from sample to sample. Although we want to know a population parameter, we observe only samples obtained from the population. Hence, we have to estimate the population parameter from a statistic. To do this, we have to know the distribution of the statistic, such as the u or the t-distribution. The method of statistical inference is illustrated in Figure 9.1.

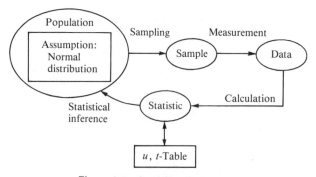

Figure 9.1   Statistical Inference

9.2 Distribution of Statistics

In statistical inference, we must know the distribution of various statistics. These can be derived from a sampling experiment. Using a computer, we generate a set of 5 random variables from $N(50, 2^2)$, and calculate $\bar{x}$, R, V, s, u and t, where

$$u = \frac{\bar{x} - \mu}{\sigma/\sqrt{n}} = \frac{\bar{x} - 50}{2/\sqrt{5}} \qquad (9.1)$$

and

$$t = \frac{\bar{x} - \mu}{s/\sqrt{n}} = \frac{\bar{x} - 50}{s/\sqrt{5}} . \qquad (9.2)$$

We iterate the above calculation 10,000 times. Thus we have 10,000 observations of the statistics $\bar{x}$, R, and so on. The first 20 cases are shown in Table 9.1. The blanks in Nos. 11—20 are left as an exercise for the reader. The histograms of the 10,000 observations of the statistics are shown in Figure 9.2—Figure 9.6, from which we can see the outlines of the distribution.

Table 9.1 Part of the Results of a Sampling Experiment

$$x_1, \cdots, x_5 \sim N(50, 2^2)$$

No.	x_1	x_2	x_3	x_4	x_5	$\bar{x}$	R	V	s	u	t
1	51	55	50	47	50	50.6	8	8.30	2.88	0.67	0.47
2	52	50	49	49	51	50.2	3	1.70	1.30	0.22	0.34
3	47	51	49	52	46	49.0	6	6.50	2.55	−1.12	−0.88
4	51	50	50	47	51	49.8	4	2.70	1.64	−0.22	−0.27
5	50	51	47	51	47	49.2	4	4.20	2.05	−0.89	−0.87
6	50	53	49	51	54	51.4	5	4.30	2.07	1.57	1.51
7	49	50	50	51	51	50.2	2	0.70	0.84	0.22	0.53
8	46	47	47	49	50	47.8	4	2.70	1.64	−2.46	−2.99
9	48	49	50	50	50	49.4	2	0.80	0.89	−0.67	−1.50
10	52	50	49	53	51	51.0	4	2.50	1.58	1.12	1.41
11	49	51	51	48	53						
12	52	51	54	50	52						
13	50	49	48	52	51						
14	51	49	52	50	48						
15	51	51	49	53	48						
16	51	55	47	50	51						
17	53	48	49	53	50						
18	53	50	49	50	51						
19	46	50	50	52	50						
20	53	52	50	50	48						

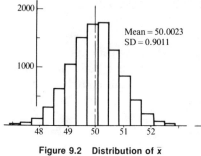

Figure 9.2   Distribution of $\bar{x}$

Mean = 50.0023
SD = 0.9011

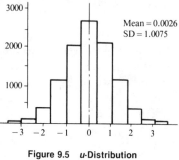

Figure 9.5 u-Distribution

Mean = 0.0026
SD = 1.0075

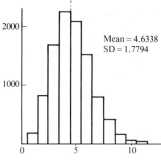

Figure 9.3   Distribution of R

Mean = 4.6338
SD = 1.7794

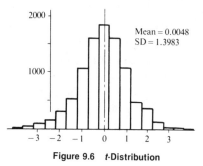

Figure 9.6 t-Distribution

Mean = 0.0048
SD = 1.3983

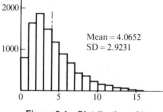

Figure 9.4   Distribution of V

Mean = 4.0652
SD = 2.9231

(1) Distribution of $\bar{x}$

From Figure 9.2, we can see that:
a) $\bar{x}$ is distributed symmetrically about the mean, giving the appearance of a normal distribution.
b) The mean of $\bar{x}$ ($= 50.0023$) is very close to the population mean ($= 50.0$).
c) The standard deviation of $\bar{x}$ ($= 0.9011$) is close to $1/\sqrt{n}$ times the population standard deviation ($2.0/\sqrt{5} = 0.8944$).

Generally, the following theorems hold:

Theorem 9.1

Suppose $x_1, \cdots, x_n$ are n observations from a population with mean μ and variance σ^2, and $\bar{x}$ is the sample mean. Then the expectation, the variance, and the standard deviation of $\bar{x}$ are

$$E(\bar{x}) = \mu, \tag{9.3}$$

$$V(\bar{x}) = \frac{\sigma^2}{n}, \tag{9.4}$$

and

$$D(\bar{x}) = \frac{\sigma}{\sqrt{n}}, \tag{9.5}$$

respectively.

Theorem 9.2

Suppose $x_1, \ldots, x_n$ are from $N(\mu, \sigma^2)$, and $\bar{x}$ is the sample mean. Then $\bar{x}$ is distributed as $N(\mu, \sigma^2/n)$.

Theorem 9.1 is directly derived from Section 8.4. It is an important fact that the standard deviation of a sample mean is $1/\sqrt{n}$ times that of the population (Figure 9.7). The precision of the sample mean $\bar{x}$ as an estimate for the population mean is proportional to the square root of the sample size, $\sqrt{n}$.

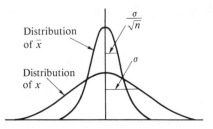

Figure 9.7   Distributions of $\bar{x}$ and x

Another important theorem on the sample mean is the *central limit theorem*, stated as follows:

Theorem 9.3 (Central Limit Theorem)────────────

The distribution of the sample mean from a population which has a finite variance, tends to a normal distribution as the sample size tends to infinity.

According to Theorem 9.2, the sample mean from a normally distributed population is exactly distributed as a normal distribution. And Theorem 9.3 says that even if the distribution of a population is not normal, the sample mean is approximately normally distributed. The approximation holds best for large values of n, but is adequate for a value of n as low as 5. For example, Figure 9.8 shows the distributions of a sample mean of n observations taken from the uniform distribution. It is due to the central limit theorem that we can make various statistical inferences using the sample mean on the assumption that the population is normally distributed.

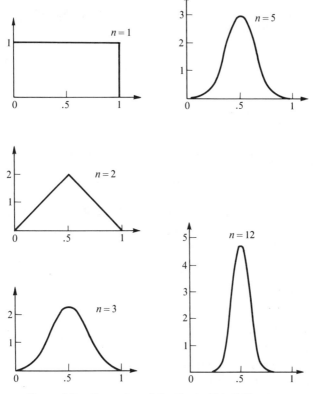

Figure 9.8   Examples of the Central Limit Theorem

(2) Distribution of *R*

From Figure 9.3, we can see that:
a) The distribution is positively skewed.
b) The mean (= 4.6338) is about 2.3 times the population standard deviation.
c) The standard deviation (= 1.7794) is about 0.9 times the population standard deviation.

Generally, the following theorem holds:

Theorem 9.4

Let R be the range of a sample $(x_1, \cdots, x_n)$ from $N(\mu, \sigma^2)$. The expectation and the standard deviation of R are

$$E(R) = d_2\sigma, \tag{9.6}$$

and

$$D(R) = d_3\sigma, \tag{9.7}$$

respectively, where d_2 and d_3 are certain constants that depend upon n.

The values of d_2 and d_3 are shown in Table A.2 of the Appendix. From the table, in this case, $n = 5$, $d_2 = 2.326$ and $d_3 = 0.864$. From the theorem, we can estimate σ from

$$\hat{\sigma} = \frac{R}{d_2} . \tag{9.8}$$

(3) Distribution of V

From Figure 9.4, we see that:
a) The distribution is positively skewed.
b) The mean ($= 4.0652$) is nearly equal to the population variance ($2.0^2 = 4.0$).
c) The standard deviation ($= 2.9231$) is about 0.7 times the population variance.

Generally, the following theorem holds:

Theorem 9.5

Let V be the variance of a sample $(x_1, \cdots, x_n)$ from $N(\mu, \sigma^2)$. The expectation and the standard deviation of V are

$$E(V) = \sigma^2 , \tag{9.9}$$

and

$$D(V) = \sqrt{\frac{2}{n-1}}\, \sigma^2 . \tag{9.10}$$

The statistic V is used for estimating the population variance σ^2. From (9.9), its expectation is equal to σ^2. An estimator whose expectation is equal to the estimated population parameter is called an *unbiased estimator*. Thus V is an unbiased estimator for σ^2. Of course, $\bar{x}$ is also an unbiased estimator for μ.

Incidentally, V is obtained by dividing the sum of the squares of the deviations S by $(n-1)$, as defined in (5.4). It may seem strange to divide S by $(n-1)$ instead of n, and one reason for this is the property (9.9). The other reason is that the number of independent variables used in calculating S is $(n-1)$. For example, when $n=1$, whatever the value of x_1 is, we have $S=0$. Hence, for a sample with $n=1$, we have no information on the variation. We can obtain information about the variation only when $n \geq 2$, and n observations contain information on $(n-1)$ variables. This number is called the *degree of freedom*. Denoting it by ϕ, in this case we have

$$\phi = n - 1. \tag{9.11}$$

(4) *u*-Distribution

Theorem 9.6

Let $\bar{x}$ be the mean of a sample $(x_1, \cdots, x_n)$ from $N(\mu, \sigma^2)$. Then the statistic

$$u = \frac{\bar{x} - \mu}{\sigma/\sqrt{n}} \tag{9.12}$$

is distributed as the standard normal distribution.

This theorem is easily derived from Theorem 9.2 and the standardization of the normal variate.

We denote the two-sided α-percentage point of the standard normal distribution by $u(\alpha)$. Namely,

$$\Pr\{|u| \geqq u(\alpha)\} = \alpha, \tag{9.13}$$

where u is distributed as $N(0, 1^2)$.

The u-distribution is used for the test and estimation of a population mean when σ is known.

(5) t-Distribution

From Figures 9.5 and 9.6, we see that the distribution of the statistic t is similar to that of u, but has a slightly larger variation.

Mathematically, the following has been established.

Theorem 9.7

In (9.12), replacing σ by the sample standard deviation s, we have

$$t = \frac{\bar{x} - \mu}{s/\sqrt{n}}. \tag{9.14}$$

t is distributed as the t-distribution with degree of freedom $\phi = n-1$.

Since σ is replaced by its estimate, it is natural for the t-distribution to have a larger variation than the standard normal distribution. When the degree of freedom, $\phi = n-1$, is small, the distribution has long tails. If n is very large, s will be very close to σ. So we might believe that for large n the distribution of t will differ little from the standard normal distribution. In fact, a t-distribution with degree of freedom $\phi = \infty$ conforms to the standard normal distribution.

The t-distribution is uniquely determined by the degree of freedom ϕ, and it is shown in Figure 9.9. We denote the two-sided α-percentage point of the t-distribution with degree of freedom ϕ by $t(\phi, \alpha)$, i.e.,

$$\Pr\{|t| \geqq t(\phi, \alpha)\} = \alpha \tag{9.15}$$

where t is distributed as a t-distribution with degree of freedom ϕ. Table A.3 of the Appendix gives the percentage points.

The t-distribution is used for the test and estimation of a population mean when σ is not known, or for the test and estimation of a difference between two population means.

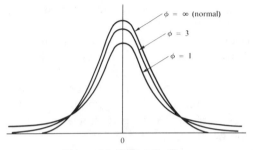

Figure 9.9   *t*-Distribution

9.3   Test of Hypothesis

Example 9.1
The tensile strength of the stainless steel produced in a certain plant has previously been stable with a mean strength of 72 kg/mm² and a standard deviation of 2.0 kg/mm². Recently, a machine was adjusted. To determine the effect of the adjustment, ten samples were tested as shown below.

Sample No. i	Strength x_i (kg/mm²)
1	76.2
2	78.3
3	76.4
4	74.7
5	72.6
6	78.4
7	75.7
8	70.2
9	73.3
10	74.2

Assume the standard deviation is the same as before the adjustment. Can we conclude that the adjustment has changed the tensile strength of the steel?

First let us make clear the meaning of the question:
1) Before the adjustment, the tensile strength of the steel is distributed as $N(\mu_0, \sigma_0^2)$. Here μ_0 and σ_0 are known as $\mu_0 = 72.0$ and $\sigma_0 = 2.0$, respectively.
2) After the adjustment, the strength is distributed as $N(\mu, \sigma^2)$, where σ is assumed to be the same as $\sigma_0 = 2.0$, but μ is not known.
3) The question is whether μ is equal to μ_0 or not. Namely, this is a problem of the comparison of two population means μ_0 and μ.
4) Ten samples are random samples form $N(\mu, \sigma^2)$. They have some information on μ.

Taking the mean $\bar{x}$ of the 10 samples, we have

$$\bar{x} = \frac{76.2 + \cdots + 74.2}{10} = 75.0 . \qquad (9.16)$$

This value is different from the mean before the adjustment, $\mu_0 = 72.0$ kg/mm². However, we cannot conclude from this that the adjustment has changed the strength of the steel, because the sample mean $\bar{x}$ has a variation and is not always equal to the population mean.

Let us consider a hypothesis that the adjustment has not changed the strength of the steel. If this hypothesis were true, then $\bar{x}$ would be normally distributed with mean $\mu_0 = 72.0$ and standard deviation

$$\sigma/\sqrt{n} = 2.0/\sqrt{10} = 0.632.$$

Hence the standardized variable u_0 given by

$$u_0 = \frac{\bar{x} - \mu_0}{\sigma/\sqrt{n}} = \frac{\bar{x} - 72.0}{0.632} \qquad (9.17)$$

is distributed as $N(0, 1^2)$. Since we have $\bar{x} = 75.0$ from (9.16), the value of u_0 is

$$u_0 = \frac{75.0 - 72.0}{0.632} = 4.74 . \qquad (9.18)$$

The probability of $|u_0|$ being as large as 4.74 is very small

($\fallingdotseq 0.000002$). This means either that a very unlikely event has occurred, or that the hypothesis is incorrect. We would therefore suspect that the hypothesis, $\mu = \mu_0$ ($= 72.0$), is not true. Deciding from a sample of observations whether a hypothesis on a population parameter, such as $\mu = \mu_0$ ($= 72.0$), is correct or not, is called a *test of hypothesis*.

When we consider that the hypothesis is not correct, we say that we *reject* it. In the example, when the hypothesis $H_0 : \mu = 72.0$ is true, u_0 is likely to fall near zero. So when $|u_0|$ is greater than a certain limit, we reject H_0. For example, we can follow the procedure:
  "When $|u_0| \geqq 1.96$, reject H_0,
  and when $|u_0| < 1.96$, accept H_0."
Following this, the probability of rejecting H_0 when it is true, is

$$\Pr(|u_0| \geqq 1.96) = 0.05. \tag{9.19}$$

This probability is called a *significance level*, and it is usually denoted by α. This type of error, in which a hypothesis is incorrectly rejected, is called an *error of the first kind*. The value of α is usually chosen as 0.05 (5%) or 0.01 (1%). The region of u_0 in which the hypothesis H_0 is rejected is called the *rejection region*, and the region where H_0 is accepted is called the *acceptance region*.

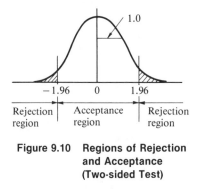

**Figure 9.10 Regions of Rejection
and Acceptance
(Two-sided Test)**

When a hypothesis is rejected, it can be said with strong conviction that "the value of parameter specified in the hypothesis is not correct." On the other hand, even if we accept a hypothesis, we cannot conclude unequivocally that the hypothesis is correct, because many other hypotheses could be accepted for the given sample of observations, and yet only one hypothesis can be true. When we accept a hypothesis which is actually not true, this error is called an *error of the second kind*, and its probability is denoted by β. When $\mu \neq \mu_0$, writing

$$u_1 = \frac{\bar{x} - \mu_0}{\sigma/\sqrt{n}} \, , \tag{9.20}$$

the probability of error of the second kind is illustrated in Figure 9.11. When a hypothesis is not true, we want to reject it with a high probability. The probability of rejecting an untrue hypothesis is called *power of test*, and is denoted by P, where $P = 1 - \beta$. The value of P varies according to the difference between μ and μ_0, as shown in Figure 9.12.

The procedure for testing a hypothesis is shown in Table 9.2.

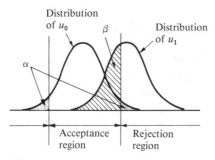

Figure 9.11   Error of the Second Kind, β

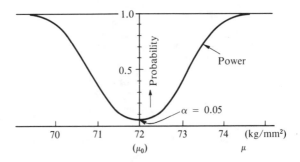

Figure 9.12   Power Curve for Example 9.1

Table 9.2 Test and Estimation of a Population Mean When σ Is Known

Procedure	Example (*Example 9.1*)
1. Hypothesis, significance level $H_0 : \mu = \mu_0$ $H_1 : \mu \neq \mu_0 \ (\alpha = 0.05 \text{ or } 0.01)$	1. Hypothesis, significance level $H_0 : \mu = \mu_0 \ (= 72.0)$ $H_1 : \mu \neq \mu_0 \ (= 72.0) \ (\alpha = 0.05)$
2. Statistics $\bar{x} = \dfrac{1}{n} \Sigma x_i$ $u_0 = \dfrac{\bar{x} - \mu_0}{\sigma/\sqrt{n}}$	2. Statistics $\bar{x} = \dfrac{1}{10} \ (76.2 + \cdots + 74.2) = 75.0$ $u_0 = \dfrac{75.0 - 72.0}{2/\sqrt{10}} = 4.74$
3. Test Obtain $u(\alpha)$ from the normal distribution table. If $|u_0| \geqq u(\alpha) \rightarrow$ reject H_0. If $|u_0| < u(\alpha) \rightarrow$ accept H_0.	3. Test $u(0.05) = 1.96$ $|u_0| = 4.74 > 1.96 = u(0.05)$ $\rightarrow$ reject H_0.
4. Estimation $\hat{\mu} = \bar{x}$ $\mu = \bar{x} \pm u\,(\alpha) \ \dfrac{\sigma}{\sqrt{n}}$	4. Estimation $\hat{\mu} = \bar{x} = 75.0$ (kg/mm^2) $\mu = 75.0 \pm 1.96 \times \dfrac{2.0}{\sqrt{10}}$ $= 75.0 \pm 1.24$ (kg/mm^2)
5. Conclusion	5. Conclusion It should be concluded, at 5% significance level, that the machine adjustment has changed the tensile strength of the steel. The 95% confidence limits for the mean are 75.0 ± 1.24 kg/mm^2.

Example 9.2
In Example 9.1, can we consider that adjustment of the machine has increased the strength of the steel? Assume the other conditions remain the same.

In Example 9.1, our concern was whether adjusting the machine had changed the strength or not. When the hypothesis $H_0 : \mu = 72.0$ was rejected, we considered that $\mu \neq 72.0$. In this example, our question is whether the adjustment has increased the strength or not. If the hypothesis were rejected, we would consider that $\mu > 72.0$.

When a hypothesis H_0 is rejected, the hypothesis we accept is called the *alternative hypothesis*, and is denoted by H_1. In Example 9.1, it was

$$H_1 : \mu \neq \mu_0 \ (= 72.0), \tag{9.21}$$

while in Example 9.2, it is

$$H_1 : \mu > \mu_0 \ (= 72.0). \tag{9.22}$$

The hypothesis H_0 is also called a *null hypothesis*, as opposed to the alternative hypothesis.

In testing the alternative hypothesis (9.21), the rejection region lies in both tails of the distribution, as shown in Figure 9.10. For (9.22), on the other hand, the rejection region lies in the right-hand tail, as shown in Figure 9.13. The former test is called a *two-sided test* and the latter a *one-sided test*.

The procedure for Example 9.2 is shown in Table 9.3.

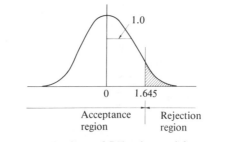

1.0

0   1.645

Acceptance | Rejection
region | region

Figure 9.13   Regions of Rejection and Acceptance (One-sided Test)

Table 9.3 Test and Estimation of a Poulation Mean (One-sided Test)

Procedure	Example (*Example 9.2*)
1. Hypothesis, significance level $H_0 : \mu = \mu_0$ $H_1 : \mu > \mu_0$ ($\alpha = 0.05$ or 0.01) (or $H_1 : \mu < \mu_0$)	1. Hypothesis, significance level $H_0 : \mu = \mu_0$ ($= 72.0$) $H_1 : \mu > \mu_0$ ($= 72.0$) ($\alpha = 0.05$)
2. Statistics As in Example 9.1.	2. Statistics As in Example 9.1.
3. Test Obtain $u(2\alpha)$ from the normal distribution table. When $H_1 : \mu > \mu_0$, if $u_0 \geqq u(2\alpha) \rightarrow$ reject H_0, if $u_0 < u(2\alpha) \rightarrow$ accept H_0. When $H_1 : \mu < \mu_0$, if $u_0 \leqq -u(2\alpha) \rightarrow$ reject H_0, if $u_0 > -u(2\alpha) \rightarrow$ accept H_0.	3. Test $u(0.10) = 1.645$ $u_0 = 4.74 > 1.645 = u(0.10)$ $\rightarrow$ reject H_0.
4. Estimation As in Example 9.1.	4. Estimation As in Example 9.1.
5. Conclusion	5. Conclusion It should be concluded, at 5% significance level, that adjusting the machine has increased the strength of the steel. The 95% confidence limits for the mean are 75.0 ± 1.24 kg/mm².

9.4   Estimation of Parameters

Example 9.3
In Example 9.1, we concluded that the mean of the strength has changed. Then, what is the value of the new population mean?

Estimation is the process of analyzing a sample to predict the corresponding value of the population parameter. A *point estimate* is an estimate of a population parameter given by a single value. The point estimate of a parameter θ is denoted by $\hat{\theta}$. For example, the population mean μ in Example 9.1 is estimated by $\bar{x}$,

$$\hat{\mu} = \bar{x} = 75.0 \, (\text{kg/mm}^2) . \qquad (9.23)$$

An *interval estimate* is an estimate of a population parameter given by two values between which the parameter is considered to lie.
Supposing $x_1, x_2, \cdots, x_n$ are from $N(\mu, \sigma^2)$, the sample mean $\bar{x}$ is distributed as $N(\mu, \frac{\sigma^2}{n})$.
Writing

$$u = \frac{\bar{x} - \mu}{\sigma/\sqrt{n}} , \qquad (9.24)$$

the distribution of u is $N(0, 1^2)$. Therefore the probability that u will fall between $\pm u(\alpha)$ is equal to $1 - \alpha$, where $u(\alpha)$ denotes the two-sided α-percentage point of the standard normal distribution. Or,

$$\Pr \left\{ -u(\alpha) < \frac{\bar{x} - \mu}{\sigma/\sqrt{n}} < u(\alpha) \right\} = 1 - \alpha . \qquad (9.25)$$

Rearranging (9.25), we have

$$\Pr \left\{ \bar{x} - u(\alpha) \frac{\sigma}{\sqrt{n}} < \mu < \bar{x} + u(\alpha) \frac{\sigma}{\sqrt{n}} \right\}$$

$$= 1 - \alpha . \qquad (9.26)$$

This interval is called the $100(1 - \alpha)\%$ *confidence interval* for μ, and the upper and lower boundaries of the interval are called *confidence limits*. (9.26) means that the probability of the interval covering μ is

$1 - \alpha$. This probability, say $(1 - \alpha)$, is called the *confidence level*. Usually the confidence level is chosen as 0.95 or 0.99. Choosing 0.95, from (9.26), the 95% confidence limits are

$$\bar{x} \pm 1.96 \frac{\sigma}{\sqrt{n}} \; . \tag{9.27}$$

The answer to Example 9.3 is shown in Step 4 of Table 9.2.

9.5 Tests and Estimations of Population Means When σ Is Not Known

Depending on the problems, other kinds of tests and estimations can be considered. The basic concepts and procedures are almost the same as described in previous sections except for the statistics used. Some common tests and estimations will be explained in the followings. At first, in this section, we will discuss the test and estimation of a population mean when σ is not known.

Suppose n samples $x_1, x_2, \cdots, x_n$ are from a population with mean μ and standard deviation σ. Then the sampling distribution of

$$u = \frac{\bar{x} - \mu}{\sigma / \sqrt{n}} \tag{9.28}$$

can be regarded as the standard normal distribution. This is applied to the test and estimation of a population mean when σ is known. However, it sometimes happens that σ is not known. In such a case, it seems natural to replace σ with s and use

$$t = \frac{\bar{x} - \mu}{s / \sqrt{n}} \tag{9.29}$$

instead of u, where s is the sample standard deviation,

$$s = \sqrt{\frac{\Sigma (x_i - \bar{x})^2}{n - 1}} \; . \tag{9.30}$$

In order to use this statistic for test and estimation, we must know the sampling distribution of t. This distribution is known as the t-distribution with $(n - 1)$ degrees of freedom.

For testing a hypothesis,

$$H_0 : \mu = \mu_0,$$
$$H_1 : \mu \neq \mu_0, \qquad\qquad (9.31)$$

calculate t_0 from

$$t_0 = \frac{\bar{x} - \mu_0}{s/\sqrt{n}}, \qquad\qquad (9.32)$$

and compare it with $t(n-1, \alpha)$, where $t(n-1, \alpha)$ denotes the two-sided α-percentage point of the t-distribution with $(n-1)$ degrees of freedom. When $|t_0| \geq t(n-1, \alpha)$, reject H_0, and when $|t_0| < t(n-1, \alpha)$, accept H_0. In the case of a one-sided test, i.e., $H_1 : \mu > \mu_0$ or $H_1 : \mu < \mu_0$, t_0 is compared with $t(n-1, 2\alpha)$ or $-t(n-1, 2\alpha)$ respectively.

Since the value of t defined in (9.29) is distributed as a t-distribution with $\phi = n-1$, we have

$$\Pr\{-t(n-1, \alpha) < t < t(n-1, \alpha)\} = 1-\alpha. \qquad\qquad (9.33)$$

Substituting $\dfrac{\bar{x} - \mu}{s/\sqrt{n}}$ for t in (9.33) and rearranging, we then obtain

$$\Pr\left\{ \bar{x} - t(n-1, \alpha)\, \frac{s}{\sqrt{n}} < \mu \right.$$
$$\left. < \bar{x} + t(n-1, \alpha)\frac{s}{\sqrt{n}} \right\} = 1 - \alpha. \qquad\qquad (9.34)$$

The 95% confidence limits of μ are

$$\bar{x} \pm t(n-1, 0.05)\frac{s}{\sqrt{n}}. \qquad\qquad (9.35)$$

An example and the procedure for analysis are shown in Table 9.4.

Table 9.4 Test and Estimation of a Population Mean When σ Is Not Known

Example 9.4

Suppose, in Example 9.1, it cannot be assumed that the standard deviation of the strength after the adjustment is the same as before. Can we believe that the adjustment has changed the strength of the steel?

Procedure	Example
1. Hypothesis, significance level $H_0 : \mu = \mu_0$ $H_1 : \mu \neq \mu_0$ ($\alpha = 0.05$ or 0.01) 2. Statistics $\bar{x} = \dfrac{1}{n}\,\Sigma x_i$ $S = \Sigma x_i^2 - \dfrac{(\Sigma x_i)^2}{n}$ $s = \sqrt{\dfrac{S}{n-1}}$ $t_0 = \dfrac{\bar{x} - \mu_0}{s/\sqrt{n}}$ 3. Test Obtain the value of $t(n-1, \alpha)$ from the t-table. If $\|t_0\| \geqq t(n-1, \alpha) \rightarrow$ reject H_0. If $\|t_0\| < t(n-1, \alpha) \rightarrow$ accept H_0.	1. Hypothesis, significance level $H_0 : \mu = \mu_0$ ($=72.0$) $H_1 : \mu \neq \mu_0$ ($\alpha = 0.05$) 2. Statistics $\Sigma x_i = 750.0$ $\Sigma x_i^2 = 56308.76$ $\bar{x} = 75.0$ $S = 56308.76 - \dfrac{750.0^2}{10} = 58.76$ $s = \sqrt{\dfrac{58.76}{9}} = \sqrt{6.53} = 2.56$ $t_0 = \dfrac{75.0 - 72.0}{2.56/\sqrt{10}} = 3.71$ 3. Test $t(9, 0.05) = 2.262$ $\|t_0\| = 3.71 > 2.262 = t(9, 0.05)$ $\rightarrow$ reject H_0.

4. Estimation

$$\hat{\mu} = \bar{x}$$

$$\mu = \bar{x} \pm t(n - 1, \alpha) \, \frac{s}{\sqrt{n}}$$

5. Conclusion

4. Estimation

$$\hat{\mu} = 75.0$$

$$\mu = 75.0 \pm 2.262 \times \frac{2.56}{\sqrt{10}} = 75.0 \pm 1.83 \ (\mathrm{kg/mm^2})$$

5. Conclusion

It should be concluded at 5% significance level, that the adjustment of the machine has changed the strength of the steel. The 95% confidence limits for the mean are 75.0 ± 1.83 kg/mm².

9.6 Tests and Estimations of the Differences Between Two Population Means

Suppose we have two sets of samples and we want to know whether the means of the two populations are equal or not.

Let $x_{11}, x_{12}, \cdots, x_{1n_1}$ be n_1 samples from the first population with mean μ_1 and standard deviation σ, and $x_{21}, x_{22}, \cdots, x_{2n_2}$ be n_2 samples from the second population with mean μ_2 and stadnard deviation σ. To test the difference between two population means, we examine the difference $\bar{x}_1 - \bar{x}_2$. Since the distributions of sample means $\bar{x}_1$ and $\bar{x}_2$ can be regarded as $N(\mu_1, \frac{\sigma^2}{n_1})$ and $N(\mu_2, \frac{\sigma^2}{n_2})$, respectively, $\bar{x}_1 - \bar{x}_2$ has a normal distribution, $N(\mu_1 - \mu_2, (\frac{1}{n_1} + \frac{1}{n_2})\sigma^2)$.

Hence, standardizing this,

$$u = \frac{(\bar{x}_1 - \bar{x}_2) - (\mu_1 - \mu_2)}{\sigma\sqrt{\frac{1}{n_1} + \frac{1}{n_2}}} \tag{9.36}$$

is distributed as $N(0, 1^2)$. Now let us assume that σ is not known. Replacing σ by s in (9.36), we have

$$t = \frac{(\bar{x}_1 - \bar{x}_2) - (\mu_1 - \mu_2)}{s\sqrt{\frac{1}{n_1} + \frac{1}{n_2}}} \tag{9.37}$$

where

$$s = \sqrt{\frac{S_1 + S_2}{n_1 + n_2 - 2}} \tag{9.38}$$

and S_1 or S_2 is the sum of the squares in each sample. t in (9.37) has a t-distribution with $\phi = n_1 + n_2 - 2$. If there is no difference between the two means, putting $\mu_1 = \mu_2$ in (9.37), we have

$$t_0 = \frac{\bar{x}_1 - \bar{x}_2}{s\sqrt{\frac{1}{n_1} + \frac{1}{n_2}}}. \tag{9.39}$$

An example and the procedure for analysis are shown in Table 9.5.

Table 9.5 Test and Estimation of the Difference Between Two Population Means

Example 9.5
The effect of welding current on breaking strength was studied.

x_1 (600A)	37	29	35	28	24	36	40	37	33	28	39		
x_2 (800A)	22	32	27	30	24	34	32	20	24	25	28	26	26

Is there any difference in the breaking strength of the welds produced using these two currents?

Procedure	Example

Procedure

1. Hypothesis, significance level
$H_0: \mu_1 = \mu_2$
$H_1: \mu_1 \neq \mu_2$ ($\alpha = 0.05$ or 0.01)

2. Statistics

$$\bar{x}_1 = \frac{1}{n_1}\Sigma x_{1i}$$

$$\bar{x}_2 = \frac{1}{n_2}\Sigma x_{2i}$$

$$S_1 = \Sigma x_{1i}^2 - \frac{(\Sigma x_{1i})^2}{n_1}$$

$$S_2 = \Sigma x_{2i}^2 - \frac{(\Sigma x_{2i})^2}{n_2}$$

Example

1. Hypothesis, significance level
$H_0: \mu_1 = \mu_2$
$H_1: \mu_1 \neq \mu_2$ ($\alpha = 0.05$)

2. Statistics

$\Sigma x_{1i} = 366$

$\Sigma x_{1i}^2 = 12454$

$\Sigma x_{2i} = 350$

$\Sigma x_{2i}^2 = 9630$

$\bar{x}_1 = \dfrac{366}{11} = 33.27$

$\bar{x}_2 = \dfrac{350}{13} = 26.92$

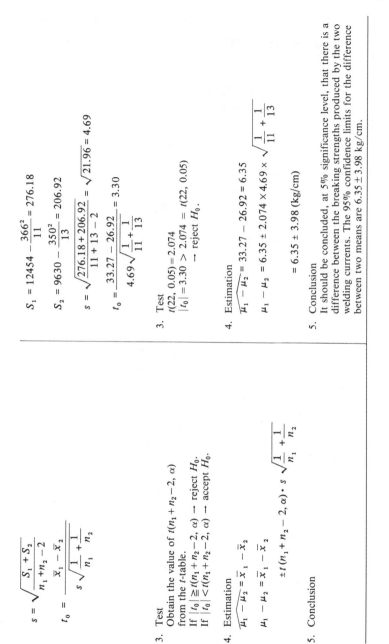

$$s = \sqrt{\frac{S_1 + S_2}{n_1 + n_2 - 2}}$$

$$t_0 = \frac{\bar{x}_1 - \bar{x}_2}{s\sqrt{\dfrac{1}{n_1} + \dfrac{1}{n_2}}}$$

3. Test

Obtain the value of $t(n_1 + n_2 - 2, \alpha)$ from the t-table.

If $|t_0| \geqq t(n_1 + n_2 - 2, \alpha) \rightarrow$ reject H_0.

If $|t_0| < t(n_1 + n_2 - 2, \alpha) \rightarrow$ accept H_0.

4. Estimation

$$\widehat{\mu_1 - \mu_2} = \bar{x}_1 - \bar{x}_2$$

$$\mu_1 - \mu_2 = \bar{x}_1 - \bar{x}_2 \pm t(n_1 + n_2 - 2, \alpha) \cdot s \sqrt{\frac{1}{n_1} + \frac{1}{n_2}}$$

5. Conclusion

$$S_1 = 12454 - \frac{366^2}{11} = 276.18$$

$$S_2 = 9630 - \frac{350^2}{13} = 206.92$$

$$s = \sqrt{\frac{276.18 + 206.92}{11 + 13 - 2}} = \sqrt{21.96} = 4.69$$

$$t_0 = \frac{33.27 - 26.92}{4.69\sqrt{\dfrac{1}{11} + \dfrac{1}{13}}} = 3.30$$

3. Test

$t(22, 0.05) = 2.074$

$|t_0| = 3.30 > 2.074 = t(22, 0.05)$

$\rightarrow$ reject H_0.

4. Estimation

$$\widehat{\mu_1 - \mu_2} = 33.27 - 26.92 = 6.35$$

$$\mu_1 - \mu_2 = 6.35 \pm 2.074 \times 4.69 \times \sqrt{\frac{1}{11} + \frac{1}{13}}$$

$$= 6.35 \pm 3.98 \text{ (kg/cm)}$$

5. Conclusion

It should be concluded, at 5% significance level, that there is a difference between the breaking strengths produced by the two welding currents. The 95% confidence limits for the difference between two means are 6.35 ± 3.98 kg/cm.

9.7   Tests and Estimations in Paired Observations

In sampling from two populations, extraneous factors sometimes cause a significant difference in the means, whereas there is no difference in the effect we are trying to measure. For example, in an experiment to test which of two types (A or B) of fertilizers is the better, two plots of wheat are planted at each of 10 experimental stations. One of the two plots is fertilized with fertilizer A and the other with fertilizer B. If the average of 10 observations with type A is compared with the average of 10 observations with type B, the difference observed (if any) may be due to the different type of soil or different weather conditions instead of any difference between the fertilizers themselves. There is also the further possibility that the fertilizers cause a difference but that this difference is obscured by other factors. A type of experiment which can overcome these difficulties is that observations are taken in pairs. We try to make sure that the two members of any pair are alike in all respects except the one we are trying to measure. Thus each pair of plots would have almost the same type of soil, weather conditions, and so on.

Let x_{1i} be the first member of the ith pair and x_{2i} the second. We have, say, n pairs of observations,

$$(x_{11}, x_{21}), (x_{12}, x_{22}),\ldots, (x_{1i}, x_{2i}),\ldots, (x_{1n}, x_{2n}). \qquad (9.40)$$

If we take the differences $d_i = x_{1i} - x_{2i}$, we obtain a set of n observations d_i. We wish to test the hypothesis that $\mu_1 = \mu_2$. This hypothesis states that there is no difference between treatments, i.e., no difference within pairs. There may be a difference among pairs, but this can be eliminated by taking the difference d_i. If the hypothesis is true, the values of d_i would come from a population with mean zero. The test is carried out in exactly the same way as in Section 9.5 (t-test with $\phi = n-1$).

An example and the procedure for analysis are shown in Table 9.6.

Table 9.6 Test and Estimation in Paired Observations

Example 9.6
The lengths of 10 samples were measured before and after ultrasonic baking. Does the heat treatment cause a change in the length?

Sample	Before	After (mm)
1	11.94	12.00
2	11.99	11.99
3	11.98	11.95
4	12.03	12.07
5	12.03	12.03
6	11.96	11.98
7	11.95	12.03
8	11.96	12.02
9	11.92	12.01
10	12.00	11.99

Procedure	Example
1. Hypothesis, significance level $H_0 : \mu_1 - \mu_2 = 0$ $H_1 : \mu_1 - \mu_2 \neq 0$ $(\alpha = 0.05$ or $0.01)$	1. Hypothesis, significance level $H_0 : \mu_1 - \mu_2 = 0$ $H_1 : \mu_1 - \mu_2 \neq 0$ $(\alpha = 0.05)$

2. Statistics

$$d_i = x_{1i} - x_{2i}$$

$$\bar{d} = \frac{1}{n}\Sigma d_i$$

$$s = \sqrt{\frac{\Sigma d_i^2 - \dfrac{(\Sigma d_i)^2}{n}}{n-1}}$$

$$t_0 = \frac{\bar{d}}{s/\sqrt{n}}$$

x_{1i}	x_{2i}	d_i	d_i^2
11.94	12.00	−0.06	0.0036
11.99	11.99	0.00	0.0000
11.98	11.95	0.03	0.0009
12.03	12.07	−0.04	0.0016
12.03	12.03	0.00	0.0000
11.96	11.98	−0.02	0.0004
11.95	12.03	−0.08	0.0064
11.96	12.02	−0.06	0.0036
11.92	12.01	−0.09	0.0081
12.00	11.99	0.01	0.0001
Total		−0.31	0.0247

$$\bar{d} = \frac{-0.31}{10} = -0.031$$

$$s = \sqrt{\frac{0.0247 - \dfrac{(-0.31)^2}{10}}{9}}$$

$$= \sqrt{0.0016766} = 0.0409$$

$$t_0 = \frac{-0.031}{0.0409/\sqrt{10}} = -2.40$$

3. Test

Obtain $t(n-1, \alpha)$ from the t-table.

If $|t_0| \geqq t(n-1, \alpha) \to$ reject H_0.

If $|t_0| < t(n-1, \alpha) \to$ accept H_0.

4. Estimation

$\widehat{\mu_1 - \mu_2} = \bar{d}$

$\mu_1 - \mu_2 = \bar{d} \pm t(n-1, \alpha) \dfrac{s}{\sqrt{n}}$

5. Conclusion

3. Test

$t(9, 0.05) = 2.262$

$|t_0| = 2.40 > 2.262 = t(9, 0.05)$

$\to$ reject H_0.

4. Estimation

$\widehat{\mu_1 - \mu_2} = -0.031$

$\mu_1 - \mu_2 = -0.031 \pm 2.262 \times \dfrac{0.0409}{\sqrt{10}}$

$= -0.031 \pm 0.029$ (mm)

5. Conclusion

It should be concluded, at 5% significance level, that the ultrasonic baking causes a change in the length. The 95% confidence limits for the difference in the means are -0.031 ± 0.029 mm.

9.8   Tests of Significance of Correlation Coefficients

As already studied in Chapter 6, we calculate a sample correlation coefficient r when we want to know the strength of relationship between two variables x and y. Here let us assume x and y be distributed as a bivariate normal distribution with population correlation coefficient ρ. Even when $\rho = 0$, the sample correlation coefficient r is not always equal to zero. The test whether the population coefficient ρ is equal to zero or not can be carried out applying the following theorem.

Theorem 9.8

Let (x_i, y_i), $i = 1, 2, \cdots, n$ be n samples from a bivariate normal distribution with zero correlation coefficient. Denoting the sample correlation coefficient by r,

$$t = \frac{r\sqrt{n-2}}{\sqrt{1-r^2}} \tag{9.41}$$

is distributed as t-distribution with $(n-2)$ degrees of freedom.

An example and the procedure for testing the hypothesis that a population correlation coefficient is equal to zero are shown in Table 9.7.

Table 9.7 Test of a Population Correlation Coefficient

Example 9.7
In Table 6.1 (Chapter 6, p. 70) there are 30 pairs of data of the blowing air-pressure and percent defective of plastic tank. Can we conclude that there is a correlation between these two characteristics?

Procedure	Example
1. Hypothesis, significance level $H_0: \rho = 0$ $H_1: \rho \neq 0 \ (\alpha = 0.05 \text{ or } 0.01)$	1. Hypotehsis, significance level $H_0: \rho = 0$ $H_1: \rho \neq 0 \ (\alpha = 0.05)$
2. Statistics $S(xx) = \Sigma x_i^2 - \dfrac{(\Sigma x_i)^2}{n}$ $S(yy) = \Sigma y_i^2 - \dfrac{(\Sigma y_i)^2}{n}$ $S(xy) = \Sigma x_i y_i - \dfrac{(\Sigma x_i) \cdot (\Sigma y_i)}{n}$ $r = \dfrac{S(xy)}{\sqrt{S(xx) \cdot S(yy)}}$ $t_0 = \dfrac{r\sqrt{n-2}}{\sqrt{1-r^2}}$	2. Statistics $S(xx) = 2.8787$ $S(yy) = 0.0084015$ $S(xy) = 0.091293$ $r = \dfrac{0.091293}{\sqrt{2.8787 \times 0.0084015}} = 0.587$ $t_0 = \dfrac{0.587 \times \sqrt{30-2}}{\sqrt{1-0.587^2}} = 3.837$

3. Test
   Obtain the value of $t(n-2, \alpha)$ from the t-table.
   If $|t_0| \geqq t(n-2, \alpha) \to$ reject H_0.
   If $|t_0| < t(n-2, \alpha) \to$ accept H_0.

4. Estimation
   $\hat{\rho} = r$

5. Conclusion

3. Test
   $t(28, 0.05) = 2.048$
   $|t_0| = 3.837 > 2.048 = t(28, 0.05) \to$ reject H_0.

4. Estimation
   $\hat{\rho} = r = 0.587$

5. Conclusion
   It should be concluded, at 5% significance level, that there is a correlation between the blowing air-pressure and percent defective of plastic tank. The point estimate for the correlation coefficient is 0.587.

In this chapter, we have studied the fundamental concepts and elementary techniques of statistical inference. Of course, these are not exhaustive. Besides these techniques there are more sophisticated ones the reader is recommended to study in the future. They are
1) tests and estimations with respect to population variance,
2) analysis of variance,
3) design of experiment and its analysis,
4) multiple regression analysis,
and so on.

Exercise 9.1
Explain the difference in the meanings of the following pairs of terms:
1) Population and Sample.
2) Population parameter and Statistic.
3) Errors of the first kind and the second kind.
4) Significance level and confidence level.

Exercise 9.2
Fill in the blanks in Table 9.1.

Exercise 9.3
An experiment was required to determine whether or not a certain surface treatment increased the abrasion resistance of a particular type of material. Ten test-pieces of the material were taken; five of them were treated, and the others were left untreated. The abrasion resistance of the ten specimens was then measured. The results are shown below:

Treated	Untreated
18.2	12.9
16.0	11.3
12.2	13.2
16.7	16.5
14.4	14.2

Answer the following questions.
1) Can we conclude that the treatment increased the abrasion resistance? Carry out a test of hypothesis.

2) Find the 95% confidence limits for the difference in the mean abrasion resistance between treated and untreated materials.

3) Improve the design of the above experiment, if possible.

Chapter *10*

The QC Story

The *QC Story* is a procedure for problem-solving. A problem is defined in the terms used in the QC Story as follows:
   "A problem is the undesirable result of a job."
The solution of a problem is to improve the poor result to a reasonable level. The causes of the problem are investigated from the viewpoint of the facts, and the cause and effect relationship is analyzed precisely. Unfounded decisions based on imagination or desk theory are strictly avoided, since attempts to solve problems by such decisions lead in erroneous directions, incurring failure or delay in the improvement. Countermeasures for the problem are devised and implemented to prevent the causal factors from recurring. This procedure is a kind of story or drama in the activities of quality control, and this is why people call it the QC Story.

A problem is solved according to the following seven steps:
1) **Problem:**
   Identification of the problem.
2) **Observation:**
   Recognition of the features of the problem.
3) **Analysis:**
   Finding out the main causes.
4) **Action:**
   Action to eliminate the causes.
5) **Check:**
   Confirmation of the effectiveness of the action.
6) **Standardization:**
   Permanent elimination of the causes.
7) **Conclusion:**
   Review of the activities and planning for future work.

If these seven steps are clarified and implemented in this order, the improvement activities will be logically consistent and steadily accumulated. This procedure sometimes seems to be a roundabout way of solving a problem, but in the long run it is the shortest and moreover the surest route.

Each step of the QC Story will be described in detail. Each step contains several "Activities," and the contents of these will be explained in "Notes."

10.1   Problem

Define the problem clearly.

Activities
1) Show that the problem being handled is of much greater importance than any other problems.
2) Show what the background of the problem is and what its course has been so far.
3) Express in concrete terms only the undesirable results of the poor performance. Demonstrate what the loss in performance is in the present situation and how much it should be improved.
4) Set up a theme and a target, and sub-themes if necessary.
5) Nominate a person to take charge of the task officially. When the task is carried out by a team, nominate the members and the leader.
6) Present an estimated budget for the improvement.
7) Make a schedule for the improvement.

Notes
1) Innumerable problems, large and small, surround us. With limited personnel, time and money, we have to assign priorities for selecting problems. Use as much data as possible to identify the most important problem. When you select one problem as the theme from among all the others, you must be sure of the reasons for that selection.
2) Some problems are selected according to their background or the course they have taken up to now. In these cases, the circumstances must be clearly identified. Here too, as much data should be used as possible.

Giving the reasons for solving a particular problem has no

direct bearing on problem-solving but is important in an indirect sense. The step clarifying the degree of importance is necessary. If the degree of importance is extremely high and is widely understood by many people, the problem will be dealt with seriously. This gives the problem a high possibility of being solved. On the other hand, if people do not fully understand how important a problem is, even one that is easily solved, when they are asked to solve it, their efforts will be only half-hearted, or they may even abandon the job halfway through. No improvement will take place at all. To prevent this, use charts and photographs to provide results and explanations of the poor performance.

3) It would be an unfounded leap in logic to try to describe causal factors and provide remedial action for those factors while still at the stage of determining what the problem (theme) is. Causal factors are not determined at this stage, but later in the *analysis* step. Only the results of the problem are expressed, and this must be expressed correctly in order to clarify the subject. Next, the loss in performance in the present situation and the advantages of effecting improvements are described. These steps must be carried out in order to gain common recognition of the problem from as many people as possible.

4) Indicating the bases on which the target values in the theme are set is important. Absurd targets will not be accomplished. The target value could be a fraction defective of 0%, but in most cases, values such as this are, ultimately, ideal objectives. It is very difficult to achieve such objectives and even if those objectives could be achieved, in doing so, other problems might arise. A reasonable target value should be determined considering the economic efficiency and the technical possibilities.

When the theme includes many kinds of problem, divide the theme into sub-themes for effective handling of the problem. In some cases where the whole consists of many similar parts, it would be better to choose one typical part of the whole for analysis and use it as the basis for expanding outward to encompass the whole. One part is extracted and used as the main theme and the other part is used as the sub-theme.

5) State the deadline for reaching a solution of the problem. Generally, if the necessity is well understood, the question of when the problem has to be solved will also be clear. No matter

how big the estimated value of the effect is, a problem that lacks a clearly-defined schedule will be a problem with a low level of priority.

10.2   Observation

Investigate the specific features of the problem from a wide range of different viewpoints.

Activities
1) Investigate four points (time, place, type and symptom) to discover the features of the problem.
2) Then investigate from many different points of view to discover variation in the results.
3) Go to the site and collect necessary information that cannot be put into data form.

Notes
Investigate the problem from a number of different points of view and gain a full understanding of all its features. In this step, do not touch on the causes for the occurrence of the problem, just look at the problem as it is. At first glance, this resembles the previous *problem* step. People often tend to confuse these two steps, but their purposes are totally different. The objective of the *problem* step is to recognize the importance of the problem; the objective of the *observation* step is to discover factors that are causes of the problem. The same information may sometimes be used in the two different steps, but it is used for different purposes. Skilled criminal investigators and private detectives always use a common technique: they thoroughly investigate the site of the crime before they do anything else. They obtain clues from the site on which to base their hunt for the perpetrator, and gradually tighten the noose around the suspect. If the investigator does not thoroughly appreciate the situation where the crime was committed before starting the search, he will not only fail to find the right person, but may wind up arresting a wholly innocent person. The same is true in problem-solving.

1) The clues to solving a problem lie in the problem itself. When a problem is observed from a number of different viewpoints, various phenomena in the results can be discovered. These are the special features of the problem and are the clues for problem-solving. The reason is that if there is a variation in the results there must also be a variation in the causal factors, and it is thus possible to correlate the two types of variation. Using the variation in the results to find the variation in causal factors is thus an effective way of identifying the main factors.

The best angle from which to observe a problem will differ from case to case. But no matter what the problem is, there are at least four important views from which it should be investigated. These are time, place, type and symptom.

Here is an example used in impoving the fraction defective of a particular product.

a) Investigate as follows:
   — Is there any difference in the fraction defective between morning, afternoon and evening?
   — Is there any differnece in the fraction defective from Monday to Saturday?

   We could also use a number of different time scales, such as differences from week to week or month to month, or during different seasons, periods or years.

b) Next, investigate from the viewpoint of the location of the defect in the product.
   — Is there any difference in the fraction defective between top panels, side panels and bottom panels?
   — Is there any difference in the fraction defective between the locations in which products are placed in the furnace (close to the door, near the windows, near the walls, in the middle of the furnace)?

   We could also ask questions from further viewpoints such as direction (east, west, north and south) or height (top and bottom). When products are very long, does the defect occur in the forward, middle or rear section? Does the defect occur in linear or curved sections of a product that has complicated form, or does the problem depend on area, that is area A, area B, etc.?

c) Next, make a check as to type.
   — Is there any difference in the fraction defective of products

of different types made by the same company?

— Is there any difference in the fraction defective of products of the similar type made in the past?

We can also think of other angles pertinent to type, such as specification, class, whether it is used by adults or children, or by men or women, or whether the product is for domestic or export use.

d) Finally, investigate from the viewpoint of symptom. For an example of symptoms in a defective item, let us use pinholes.

— Is there any difference in form when pinholes are observed (are they circular, elliptical, angular or of some other shape)?

— Is there any difference in the way that multiple pinholes appear (linear, curved, continuous, discontinuous, etc.)?

In addition, what are the sizes of the pinholes, under what conditions? Do they appear on certain surfaces (are they all over, or only in certain areas)? What are the characteristics of the surrounding area (changes in color or quality, or appearance of foreign objects)?

2) No matter what the problem is, the investigation must be made from the above four perspectives at least. However, these alone are not sufficient. The problem must be investigated from various viewpoints based on the characteristics of the problem. The wider the variation of results discoverd, the better.

3) Generally speaking, problem-solving should be based on data. Information not based on data, i.e., memory or imagination, can be used only for reference. Information that cannot be obtained from data, however, sometimes takes on an important role in solving problems. If possible, those involved in the investigation should be at the site; not in an office, but actually on-site. Here they can observe and obtain information that cannot be put into data form. This kind of information, which works like a catalyst in a chemical reaction, gives new hints for solving the problem during the thinking process.

10.3   Analysis

Find out what the main causes are.

Activities

1) Set up hypotheses (selecting major candidates as causes).
   a) Write down a cause-and-effect diagram (a diagram that contains all elements seemingly related to the problem) so as to collect all knowledge concerning possible causes.
   b) Use the information obtained in the *observation* step and delete any elements which are clearly not relevant. Revise the cause-and-effect diagram using the remaining elements.
   c) Mark those elements in the latter diagram which seem to have a high possibility of being main causes.
2) Test the hypotheses (derive the main causes from the candidates).
   a) From elements that have a high possibility of being causes, devise new plans to ascertain the effect that those elements have on the problem by obtaining new data or by carrying out experiments.
   b) Integrate all the information investigated and decide which are the main possible causes.
   c) If possible, intentionally reproduce the problem.

Notes

This step is divided into two parts, the first being setting up hypotheses and the second verifying those hypotheses. The reason for having these steps is that, in the QC Story, causes must be determined scientifically. In many instances, the cause of a problem is determined either through discussion among those concerned with solving the problem, or by the arbitrary decision of one person. Decisions of this type are often in error, and most of these errors occur when the step of verifying the hypotheses is skipped. When we think about causes (the hypotheses), the reasons are discussed and the data are analyzed. The illusion is likely to arise during discussion and data analysis that the data and discussion verify the correctness of a hypothesis. But the building of hypotheses and the testing of them are two different things, and the same data cannot be used for both. Verification of hypotheses requires new data not used for building hypotheses. The collection of data for testing hypotheses must be planned logically and the hypotheses should be tested by statistical procedures.

1) To set up the hypotheses, a cause-and-effect diagram is a useful tool. All the elements in the diagram are hypothetical causes of the problem. The diagram must contain the elements which will ultimately be identified as the main causes.

   a) The expression of the effect in the diagram must be as concrete as possible, since if it is expressed in abstract terms, the number of elements in the diagram will become tremendously large. However, since an abstract definition is an integration of various individual cases, each of those cases has parts that are unnecessary. For example, if we express the effect as a type of defect, the causes in the diagram will be a collection of factors causing the defect. However, if we make the effect the defectives including many types of defects, it is necessary to collect many types of defects and the content of the diagram will be diversified. Thus, the more concrete the expression of characteristics, the more effective the diagram.

      First, draw up a cause-and-effect diagram that has enough elements to include all the opinions of those involved in solving the problem.

   b) Investigating all the possible causes would not be effective, so at this point, we have to reduce their number based on the data. The information examined in the *observation* step will be very useful for this. Elements that do not correspond to the variation of results are removed from the chart.

      Say, for example, that the fraction defective is high in the morning and low in the afternoon. If the workers are the same at both times of day, we remove workers from the diagram, since they do not match the result. But if machinery used during the morning and afternoon is different, machinery is left in the diagram since it matches the result.

      If various dispersed results have been examined in the *observation* step, we can remove many of the possible causes from the diagram. After elements which cannot be causes have been removed in this way, we make another cause-and-effect diagram using the remaining elements. The smaller this diagram (the smaller the number of elements), the better.

   c) All elements in the revised diagram do not have the same

probability of causing the problem. The elements should be ranked according to their probabilities on the basis of the information obtained in the *observation* step and examined in this order.

We have thus restricted the main candidates for causes, but we must keep in mind that the candidates are still just candidates. As it stands, we cannot yet determine that the elements evaluated as having high possibilities are the main causes of the problem, because the data used so far is data that has been used to set up the hypotheses, and we have to use data derived through a new plan to determine whether or not those hypotheses are correct.

2) The tests of the hypotheses must also be based on data obtained from experiments and surveys. The data should be collected according to a carefully-constructed plan.

a) Testing the hypotheses is investigating whether a relation actually exists between the possible causes and the results, and, if it does exist, how strong the relationship is, i.e., what effect the possible cause has. There are various methods of expressing the strength of such a relationship, e.g., correlation coefficients, analysis of variance and the Pareto diagram for causes. Or, they can simply be marked in the cause-and-effect diagram.

We must avoid making decisions on main causes through "votes." Determining the main cause by vote is a democratic method, but there is no guarantee of its scientific correctness. There are many instances where an element has been selected by unanimous agreement, and, after investigation, the element was found not to be a cause.

Sometimes, remedial actions are implemented without any data analysis. All actions which seem likely to be effective are put into practice. If the results are good, the problem-solving is considered to be finished. The order is exactly the reverse of that advocated here, because what is being done is to investigate the cause by action. To solve a problem, this procedure requires a great deal of trial and error. Even if the problem is solved and even if we see that the remedial actions are effective in solving the problem, in most cases we will not be able to find out the true main causes, because the relationship between causes and remedial actions do not correspond on a one-to-one basis.

b) The main cause is one or several elements which have the greatest influence on the results. A large number of elements can influence the result in some way or another, whether major or minor, but it would be ineffective to adopt remedies for all elements. Remedial actions should be taken against factors of major causality and not against those that have a minor effect. This is why we have to investigate and integrate all kinds of information and determine what the major causes are.

c) Evidence for the cause can be found by intentional reproduction of the defect. However, such reproduction should be undertaken carefully. If we use a non-standard unit of some product, a defective product may be produced, but this does not necessarily mean that the non-standard unit is the cause of the defect. Some other factors might be the cause of the defect. A defect produced intentionally should have the same features as the defective product, as clarified in the *observation* step. Though intentional reproduction is an effective method of verifying hypotheses, there are instances when this is not permissible owing to human, social or practical (time, economic) reason. In such cases, we should be more careful in performing the *observation* and *analysis* steps.

10.4 Action

Take action to eliminate the main causes.

Activities
1) A strict distinction must be made between actions taken to cure phenomena (immediate remedy) and actions taken to eliminate causal factors (preventing recurrence).
2) Make sure that the actions do not produce other problems (side-effects). If they do, adopt other actions or devise remedies for the side-effects.
3) Devise a number of different proposals for action, examine the

advantages and disadvantages of each and select those which the people involved agree to.

Notes
1) There are two types of action. One is action for handling phenomena (results), while the other is action taken to prevent the factor causing the result from occurring again. If we produce a defective product, we will repair the product. Even if we succeed in reparing it, the repair will not prevent the defect from recurring. The ideal way of solving a problem is to prevent it from happening again by adopting remedies to eliminate the cause of the problem. The two different types of action should not be confused. Always adopt procedures that eliminate the causes.
2) Actions often cause other problems. They resemble the use of a medical treatment which cures one disease but has side-effects that give the patient yet another ailment. To prevent the side-effects, the action has to be thoroughly evaluated and judged from as wide a range of viewpoints as possible. Also, preparatory tests (experiments) should be performed on the method. If side-effects are found to arise, consider another action or a remedy for the side-effects.
3) An important practical point in selecting actions is whether or not the active cooperation of all those involved can be secured. An action attacking a causal factor will bring forth various changes in work practices. The action must be one that everyone agrees to. If there are many possible countermeasures, the advantages and disadvantages of each measure should be examined from every point of view of the people involved. In the final decision, if there are several possible solutions that satisfy economical and technical conditions equally well, it is better to select one on a democratic basis.

10.5 Check

Make sure the problem is prevented from occurring again.

Activities

1) In the same format (tables, graphs, charts), compare the data obtained on the problem (undesirable results in the theme) both before and after the actions have been taken.
2) Convert the effects into monetary terms, and compare the result with the target value.
3) If there are any other effects, good or bad, list them.

Notes

1) In the *check* step, we ask, "How well has the recurrence been prevented?" The data we should use to check the effectiveness of the actions is data taken before and after the actions have been implemented. In the *check* step, a comparison of the situations before and after the actions is carried out to determine to what degree the undesirable results have been reduced. The format used in this comparison (tables, graphs, charts) must be the same both before and after the actions. For example, if a Pareto diagram is used to indicate the status prior to implementation of the actions, then a Pareto diagram must be used to check the effectiveness of those actions.
2) In management, it is important to attempt to convert the results of the actions into monetary terms. Several important things will be discovered for management when the losses before and after the actions are compared.
3) When the result of the actions is not as satisfactory as expected, make sure that all the planned actions have been implemented precisely according to the decision. If the undesirable results continue to occur even after the actions have been taken, the problem-solving has failed, and it is necessary to go back to the *observation* step and start again.

10.6 Standardization
Eliminate the cause of the problem permanently.

Activities

1) The five W's and one H: who, when, where, what, why and how, for the improved job must be clearly identified and used as a standard.
2) Necessary preparations and communication in regard to the standards should be carried out correctly.
3) Education and training should be implemented.
4) A system of responsibility must be set up to check on whether the standards are being observed.

Notes

Remedial actions must be standardized to prevent the problem from recurring permanently. There are two main reasons for standardization. The first is that without standards, the actions taken to solve a problem will gradually revert to the old ways and lead to a recurrence of the problem. The second is that without clear standards, the problem is likely to recur when new people (new employees, transferees, or part-time workers) become involved in the work. Standardization will not be achieved simply by documents. Standards must become a part of the thoughts and habits of the workers. Education and training are needed to provide them with the knowledge and techniques to implement the standards.

1) Standardization is another way of expressing the five W's and one H for work procedures. Just showing the one H (how) may be called a standard on some occasions, and a standard may be considered satisfactory if four of the W's (except the "why") and one H are presented. The method of executing a job can be understood well without the "why." But the "why" is indispensable to the person doing the job. There are many other methods, besides the standard, of doing a job and getting results. Thus it is very likely that the worker will use a nonstandard method if he does not know why the standardized one should be used. This is why the "why" must be included in a standard. After people have understood the "why," they will observe the standards

closely. The QC Story is a good tool for understanding the "why." Thus the standards cannot be separated from the QC Story that produces them. When training and education are given on standards, the related QC Story should be studied too.

2) Lack of proper preparation and communication is one of the main reasons for confusion when new standards are introduced. Putting new standards into practice changes work practices and results in confusion produced by trivial mistakes; and sometimes problems arise, particularly in workplaces where a system of division of work is adopted, if one place is doing things by the new method and another place is still using the old method.

3) Adequate education and training are often necessary to make standards stick. If the company is remiss in conducting this training, no matter how good the standards themselves are, they will not be carried out as they should be and problems cannot be prevented from occurring again.

4) At times a problem will be solved only for the same problem to crop up later. The major cause of this is that the standards were observed at first, but eventually were allowed to lapse. A system of responsibility must be set up to check on whether standards are being observed steadfastly to prevent the recurrence of problems.

10.7 Conclusion

Review the problem-solving procedure and plan future work.

Activities
1) Sum up the problems remaining.
2) Plan what is to be done to solve those problems.
3) Think about what has gone well and badly in the improvement activities.

Notes
1) A problem is almost never perfectly solved and the ideal situation almost never exists. It is not good to aim for perfection or to con-

tinue the same activities on the same theme for too long. When the original time limit is reached, delimiting the activities is important. Even if the target is not reached, a list should be made of how far the activities have progressed and what has not been attained yet.

2) Establish plans on what to do in the future with the problems remaining. The important problems in those plans should be continued as themes in the next QC Story.

3) Finally, some reflective thinking should be given to the activities of problem-solving themselves. This will aid in upgrading the quality of subsequent improvement activities. There is always a difference between the activity actually carried out and that understood intellectually to have been carried out, and such gaps have to be filled up one by one. This review should be carried out even if the problem was successfully solved, but this "brain-practice" should be performed with particular care if the deadline has passed and the problem is not solved. The unsolved problems can then be taken up in the next stage of the QC Story.

Epilogue

Facts

The general causes of troubles in factories arise from wrong knowledge and incorrect operations.
To discern what is wrong and what is incorrect we have to launch facts-finding process.

"The facts."

An overused expression.
Everybody assumes he knows, but no one actually knows.
One might be reminded of a story of the blind men touching an elephant and each reporting different description of what the elephant is.
One touches the trunk and talks only that, another touches the tail and describes the elephant as such.
Each believes his experience to be correct.
People often tell the stories from others as if they were their own experiences.

Discussions alone cannot eliminate troubles.
Words cannot always describe facts.
What is white may turn out as black.
Discussions cannot settle whether it is white or black.

"Let facts speak themselves."

With a humble attitude, carefully check things one by one.
At any rate what we are dealing with is a difficult thing.

It has an infinite number of features.
We must be aware that our knowledge and experience are finite, and always imperfect.
This recognition will make the facts appear.

A person who has engaged in a job for a long time is the one we call experienced.
An experienced person has a great deal of knowledge about that job.
There are correct knowledge and incorrect knowledge.
The problem is that he doesn't know which is correct and which is wrong.
A true expert is the experienced person who is always furnishing his knowledge with facts, reflecting on that knowledge and making corrections.
Unfortunately, all persons with experience are not necessarily be true experts.
They can become encumbrances who bear superstitions.

We have to work diligently to find true knowledge.
It is just like in climbing a mountain road, you have to climb one step at a time.
After you've continued the climb for some time, you'll suddenly realize how far you are above the starting point.

Appendix

Table A.1 Table of Normal Distribution

Table to obtain ϵ from K_ϵ

K_ϵ	*=0	1	2	3	4	5	6	7	8	9
0.0*	.5000	.4960	.4920	.4880	.4840	.4801	.4761	.4721	.4681	.4641
0.1*	.4602	.4562	.4522	.4483	.4443	.4404	.4364	.4325	.4286	.4247
0.2*	.4207	.4168	.4129	.4090	.4052	.4013	.3974	.3936	.3897	.3859
0.3*	.3821	.3783	.3745	.3707	.3669	.3632	.3594	.3557	.3520	.3483
0.4*	.3446	.3409	.3372	.3336	.3300	.3264	.3228	.3192	.3156	.3121
0.5*	.3085	.3050	.3015	.2981	.2946	.2912	.2877	.2843	.2810	.2776
0.6*	.2743	.2709	.2676	.2643	.2611	.2578	.2546	.2514	.2483	.2451
0.7*	.2420	.2389	.2358	.2327	.2296	.2266	.2236	.2206	.2177	.2148
0.8*	.2119	.2090	.2061	.2033	.2005	.1977	.1949	.1922	.1894	.1867
0.9*	.1841	.1814	.1788	.1762	.1736	.1711	.1685	.1660	.1635	.1611
1.0*	.1587	.1562	.1539	.1515	.1492	.1469	.1446	.1423	.1401	.1379
1.1*	.1357	.1335	.1314	.1292	.1271	.1251	.1230	.1210	.1190	.1170
1.2*	.1151	.1131	.1112	.1093	.1075	.1056	.1038	.1020	.1003	.0985
1.3*	.0968	.0951	.0934	.0918	.0901	.0885	.0869	.0853	.0838	.0823
1.4*	.0808	.0793	.0778	.0764	.0749	.0735	.0721	.0708	.0694	.0681
1.5*	.0668	.0655	.0643	.0630	.0618	.0606	.0594	.0582	.0571	.0559
1.6*	.0548	.0537	.0526	.0516	.0505	.0495	.0485	.0475	.0465	.0455
1.7*	.0446	.0436	.0427	.0418	.0409	.0401	.0392	.0384	.0375	.0367
1.8*	.0359	.0351	.0344	.0336	.0329	.0322	.0314	.0307	.0301	.0294
1.9*	.0287	.0281	.0274	.0268	.0262	.0256	.0250	.0244	.0239	.0233
2.0*	.0228	.0222	.0217	.0212	.0207	.0202	.0197	.0192	.0188	.0183
2.1*	.0179	.0174	.0170	.0166	.0162	.0158	.0154	.0150	.0146	.0143
2.2*	.0139	.0136	.0132	.0129	.0125	.0122	.0119	.0116	.0113	.0110
2.3*	.0107	.0104	.0102	.0099	.0096	.0094	.0091	.0089	.0087	.0084
2.4*	.0082	.0080	.0078	.0075	.0073	.0071	.0069	.0068	.0066	.0064
2.5*	.0062	.0060	.0059	.0057	.0055	.0054	.0052	.0051	.0049	.0048
2.6*	.0047	.0045	.0044	.0043	.0041	.0040	.0039	.0038	.0037	.0036
2.7*	.0035	.0034	.0033	.0032	.0031	.0030	.0029	.0028	.0027	.0026
2.8*	.0026	.0025	.0024	.0023	.0023	.0022	.0021	.0021	.0020	.0019
2.9*	.0019	.0018	.0018	.0017	.0016	.0016	.0015	.0015	.0014	.0014
3.0*	.0013	.0013	.0013	.0012	.0012	.0011	.0011	.0011	.0010	.0010

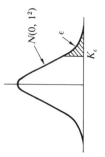

$N(0, 1^2)$

ϵ

K_ϵ

Example: The value of ϵ for $K_\epsilon = 1.96$ is obtained as follows; go to the right from 1.9* of the first column, stop at 6 of the first row, then 0.0250 is obtained.

Table A.2 Coefficients for $\bar{x}$-R Chart

Sample Size n	$\bar{x}$ Chart	R Chart				
	A_2	d_2	$1/d_2$	d_3	D_3	D_4
2	1.880	1.128	0.8862	0.853	—	3.267
3	1.023	1.693	0.5908	0.888	—	2.575
4	0.729	2.059	0.4857	0.880	—	2.282
5	0.577	2.326	0.4299	0.864	—	2.115
6	0.483	2.534	0.3946	0.848	—	2.004
7	0.419	2.704	0.3698	0.833	0.076	1.924
8	0.373	2.847	0.3512	0.820	0.136	1.864
9	0.337	2.970	0.3367	0.808	0.184	1.816
10	0.308	3.078	0.3249	0.797	0.223	1.777

Note: Symbol "—" in the column D_3 means that the LCL is not considered.

Table A.3 Percentage Points for *t*-Distribution

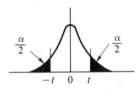

ϕ \\ α	0.10	0.05	0.02	0.01
1	6.314	12.706	31.821	63.657
2	2.920	4.303	6.965	9.925
3	2.353	3.182	4.541	5.841
4	2.132	2.776	3.747	4.604
5	2.015	2.571	3.365	4.032
6	1.943	2.447	3.143	3.707
7	1.895	2.365	2.998	3.499
8	1.860	2.306	2.896	3.355
9	1.833	2.262	2.821	3.250
10	1.812	2.228	2.764	3.169
11	1.796	2.201	2.718	3.106
12	1.782	2.179	2.681	3.055
13	1.771	2.160	2.650	3.012
14	1.761	2.145	2.624	2.977
15	1.753	2.131	2.602	2.947
16	1.746	2.120	2.583	2.921
17	1.740	2.110	2.567	2.898
18	1.734	2.101	2.552	2.878
19	1.729	2.093	2.539	2.861
20	1.725	2.086	2.528	2.845
25	1.708	2.060	2.485	2.787
30	1.697	2.042	2.457	2.750
40	1.684	2.021	2.423	2.704
60	1.671	2.000	2.390	2.660
120	1.658	1.980	2.358	2.617
∞	1.645	1.960	2.326	2.576

1) This table is used for obtaining the *t*-value when the degree of freedom (ϕ) and the two-sided probability (α) are given. For example, when $\phi = 10$ and $\alpha = 0.05$ are given, then $t = 2.228$.

2) In our notation, the value in the table is denoted by $t(\phi, \alpha)$. So $t(10, 0.05) = 2.228$.

3) When $\phi = \infty$, the values conform to the percentile values of the standard normal distribution, i.e., $t(\infty, \alpha) = u(\alpha)$.

Answers to Exercises

2.1

What the workers or the supervisors are saying may be true, but the facts should be checked with the aid of data. Data should be collected in such a way as to reveal what type of defective is prevalent and what the cause of that defective is. With this in mind, the problem should be tackled by the following steps:

1) Stratify the types of defective and find out which type is the major problem.
2) Make a list of the possible causes of that defective, for example, materials, parts, the machines themselves, tools, the operators, the method of taking measurements, etc.
3) Take data in such a way as to isolate the effect of each cause. Since in this example there are two operators and two machines, these two possible causes should at least be examined by stratification.
4) When the causes cannot be clearly stratified, records should be taken. This should be done when, for example, the materials or method of operations is changed.
5) The data should be analyzed with the aid of Pareto diagrams, check sheets, scatter diagrams, etc.
6) Once the cause of the defective is made clear, countermeasures should be taken and the results of such countermeasures should be watched carefully.

3.1

1) The overall Pareto diagram shown in the figure indicates that the defect present in the largest numbers is *strain* (•). This is also true in most of the itemized charts, so strain is the defect which we should tackle first.

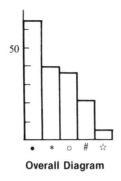

Overall Diagram

2) When we compare the two operators A and B, it is clear that A produces a larger number of defects than B. There must be some reason for this, and so we should try to analyze this situation further.

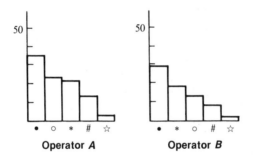

Operator A   **Operator B**

3) When we compare the four machines 1, 2, 3 and 4, we see that more defects are produced overall by machine 1 than by any other machines. But machine is operated by operator A only, and not by operator B. Thus it appears that the larger number of defective items produced by machine 1 has some bearing on the fact that operator A's overall fraction defective is larger than operator B's. Lending support to this is the fact that operator A also operates machine 2, but there is no obvious disparity between the breakdown of defects produced by this machine and those of machines 3 and 4. It seems that machine 1 is the cause of the trouble, and we should therefore investigate this further.

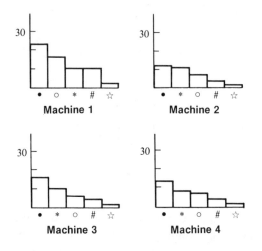

4) If we compare the numbers of defects produced on different days of the week, we see that more defects occur on Wednesday than on other days. And if we then look at the breakdown of defects for this day, it is apparent that *scratches* (*) concentrate, while the other types of defect occur in more or less the same numbers. On checking the table of raw data (Table 3.3), we see that the two operators and the four machines all produce a far larger number of scratches on Wednesday than on any other days. There must be a particular reason for this, and we should investigate it further.

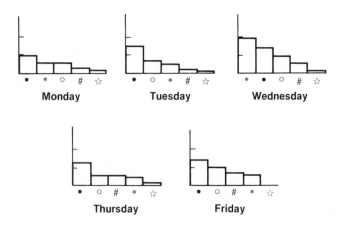

Summary:

To summarize the courses of action suggested by this analysis:

a) If machine 1 is checked, it should be possible to decrease the number of defects slightly in every category.

b) If the cause of the abnormally large number of scratches occurring on Wednesday is identified, it should be possible to decrease the number of occurrences of this particular defect.

c) If strain, the most prevalent defect overall, is made the target of investigation, it should be possible to reduce the number of defects in this category.

By tackling the problem systematically in this way, it will be possible to bring about a drastic decrease in the overall number of nonconforming items produced.

4.1

1) A cause-and-effect diagram of typing errors (mistyping).

For one solution to this problem, please refer to the figure below. However, remember that this is by no means the only possible answer. Cause-and-effect diagrams are such that for any one problem, there is a large variety of alternative solutions, and no one of them can be said to be the correct one.

2) and 3) should be tackled individually.

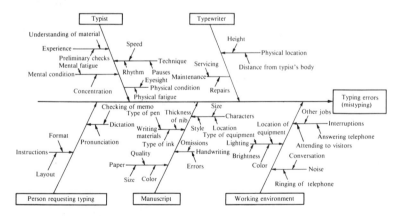

Cause-and-Effect Diagram of Typing Errors

5.1

1) For the different kinds of histograms and their statistics, see the figure and the table.
2) Remarks:
   a) All the non-conforming loaves are produced by machine 1, and from the histograms for this machine, we see that they are of the twin-peak type. Thus standard deviation, s, is large and the left-hand peak is probably causing the non-conformity. This situation should be analyzed carefully, and if the two peaks can be classified separately, it should be possible to reduce the variation in the data and decrease the non-conforming rate.
   b) In the histogram of baker A using machine 2, there is one value which is separated from the rest of the data. There is a strong possibility that this is a spurious value, and it should be checked.
   c) The means of all these histograms are smaller than the central value of the specification limits, 212.5. If the cause for this is made clear and the means are brought closer to this central value, the non-conforming rate should drop. This will not necessarily improve the variation, which is still too large, but if the actions suggested in a) and b) are successful, the variation should be brought down to a low enough value.

   If all three of the above measures are put into effect, the process will meet the specification.

Histograms

Machine 1

Bin	Baker A	Baker B	Total
193.7	0	1	1
196.2	1	2	3
198.7	1	7	8
201.2	8	7	15
203.7	7	8	15
206.2	9	3	12
208.7	9	5	14
211.2	5	3	8
213.7	0	3	3
216.2	0	1	1
218.7	0	0	0
221.2	0	0	0

Machine 2

Bin	Baker A	Baker B	Total
193.7	0	0	0
196.2	0	0	0
198.7	0	0	0
201.2	4	0	0
203.7	4	1	5
206.2	10	7	11
208.7	10	11	21
211.2	6	10	20
213.7	5	10	16
216.2	0	1	6
218.7	1	0	0
221.2	—	0	1

Total

Bin	Baker A	Baker B	Total
193.7	0	1	1
196.2	1	2	3
198.7	1	7	8
201.2	11	7	15
203.7	13	9	20
206.2	19	10	23
208.7	16	16	35
211.2	15	13	28
213.7	6	13	19
216.2	5	2	7
218.7	0	0	0
221.2	1	0	1

Note: *: product meeting specification. ≠: defective product

Values of n, $\bar{x}$ and s for Each Histogram

	Baker A	Baker B	Total
Machine 1	$n = 40$ $\bar{x} = 205.37$ $s = 3.75$	$n = 40$ $\bar{x} = 204.40$ $s = 5.38$	$n = 80$ $\bar{x} = 204.88$ $s = 4.63$
Machine 2	$n = 40$ $\bar{x} = 210.66$ $s = 4.15$	$n = 40$ $\bar{x} = 210.34$ $s = 2.89$	$n = 80$ $\bar{x} = 210.50$ $s = 3.56$
Total	$n = 80$ $\bar{x} = 208.01$ $s = 4.75$	$n = 80$ $\bar{x} = 207.37$ $s = 5.23$	$n = 160$ $\bar{x} = 207.69$ $s = 4.99$

6.1

1)

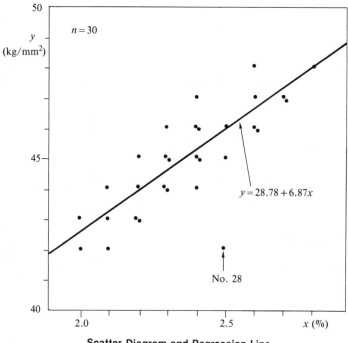

$n = 30$

$y = 28.78 + 6.87x$

No. 28

y (kg/mm^2)

x (%)

Scatter Diagram and Regression Line

a) There is a positive correlation between x and y.
b) There is a point (No.28, $x = 2.5\%$, $y = 42\text{kg/mm}^2$) which differs from other points. It should be investigated why this data has an outlying value.

2) $r = 0.789$
$r = 0.877$, when the data No. 28 is eliminated.

3) $y = 29.58 + 6.48x$.
$y = 28.78 + 6.87x$, when the data No.28 is eliminated.

7.1
1) $\bar{x}$-R
2) pn
3) c
4) x-Rs
5) p
6) $\bar{x}$-R
7) u

7.2
$\bar{\bar{x}} = 53.25$
$\bar{R} = 0.576$
Control lines

$\bar{x}$ chart UCL $= \bar{\bar{x}} + A_2\bar{R} = 53.25 + 0.729 \times 0.576 = 53.67$
CL $= \bar{\bar{x}} = 53.25$
LCL $= 52.83$

R chart UCL $= D_4\bar{R} = 2.28 \times 0.576 = 1.313$
CL $= \bar{R} = 0.576$
LCL $= $ —— (not considered)

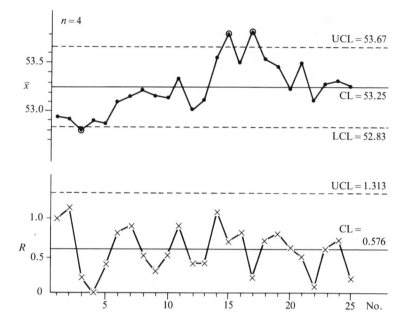

R chart shows a controlled state. However, $\bar{x}$ chart doesn't show a controlled state:

1) There are three points outside the control limits Nos. 3, 15, and 17.
2) There is a run of length 10 (Nos. 1 – 10).

Consequently this process is not in a stable state. The process mean is in lower level before Nov. 13, and it goes up and down again. We should find the cause of change in the process mean.

7.3
1) Correct.
2) Correct.
3) We should also check whether the points form some sort of particular pattern or not.
4) Correct.
5) When a point falls outside the LCL, we should consider the process is out of control. We can get useful information if we investigate the reason why the control characteristic is lower than the LCL.

6) A process in the controlled state can produce defective products.
7) In any case we should try to find the cause, when a control chart shows an uncontrolled state.
8) Correct.
9) A subgroup is possibly composed of heterogenous data. We should check the contents of within-subgroup variation, and try other ways of subgrouping.

8.1

Sum and Difference of A and B

No.	$A + B$	$A - B$
1	12.35	1.55
2	11.20	2.30
3	11.90	2.60
4	11.05	1.95
5	12.90	3.00
6	11.60	3.80
7	11.10	2.60
8	11.45	3.55
9	11.85	2.25
10	12.80	3.00

Statistics of A, B, A + B, and A − B

	A	B	$A + B$	$A - B$
Total	72.40	45.80	118.20	26.6
Sum of Square	2.279	1.951	4.096	4.364
Variance	0.253	0.217	0.455	0.485

8.2
Let preset value be c, and the weights of content and container be x, y, respectively, then

$$x + y = c + e,$$

where e is the weighing error of the machine.
The weight of content is given by

$$x = c + e - y.$$

c is a constant and e and y are independent, so the variance of x becomes the sum of the variance of y and e, that is

$$\sigma_x^2 = \sigma_1^2 + \sigma_2^2.$$

9.1

1) A population is a thing on which we take action, and a sample is a small part of the population. Based on the sample, we can estimate the characteristics of the entire population.

2) A population parameter is a constant which characterizes the population, and a statistic is a function of sample observations obtained from the population. Based on the value of the statistic, we can draw an inference about the corresponding value of the population parameter.

3) In testing a hypothesis, two types of error can be made. An error of the first kind is an error of rejecting the true hypothesis, and an error of the second kind is an error of accepting the untrue hypothesis.

4) A significance level is the probability of rejecting a hypothesis incorrectly, and a confidence level is the probability of confidence limits covering the true value of the estimated parameter.

9.2

No.	$\bar{x}$	R	V	s	u	t
11	50.4	5	3.80	1.95	0.45	0.46
12	51.8	4	2.20	1.48	2.01	2.72
13	50.0	4	2.50	1.58	0.00	0.00
14	50.0	4	2.50	1.58	0.00	0.00
15	50.4	5	3.80	1.95	0.45	0.46
16	50.8	8	8.20	2.86	0.89	0.62
17	50.6	5	5.30	2.30	0.67	0.58
18	50.6	4	2.30	1.52	0.67	0.88
19	49.6	6	4.80	2.19	−0.45	−0.41
20	50.6	5	3.80	1.95	0.67	0.69

9.3

1) 1. Hypothesis, significance level
$H_0 : \mu_1 = \mu_2$
$H_1 : \mu_1 > \mu_2 \ (\alpha = 0.05)$

2. Statistics
$\Sigma x_{1i} = 77.5$

$\Sigma x_{1i}^2 = 1222.33$

$\Sigma x_{2i} = 68.1$

$\Sigma x_{2i}^2 = 942.23$

$\bar{x}_1 = \dfrac{77.5}{5} = 15.50$

$\bar{x}_2 = \dfrac{68.1}{5} = 13.62$

$S_1 = 1222.33 - \dfrac{77.5^2}{5} = 21.08$

$S_2 = 942.23 - \dfrac{68.1^2}{5} = 14.71$

$s = \sqrt{\dfrac{21.08 + 14.71}{5 + 5 - 2}} = \sqrt{\dfrac{35.79}{8}} = \sqrt{4.474} = 2.115$

$t_0 = \dfrac{15.50 - 13.62}{2.115 \cdot \sqrt{\frac{1}{5} + \frac{1}{5}}} = \dfrac{1.88}{1.3376} = 1.405$

3. Test
$t(8, 0.10) = 1.860$
$t_0 = 1.405 < 1.860 = t(8, 0.10)$
$\rightarrow$ accept H_0.

4. Conclusion
We cannot conclude, at 5% significance level, that the treatment increased the abrasion resistance.

2) $\widehat{\mu_1 - \mu_2} = \bar{x}_1 - \bar{x}_2 = 1.88$

$$\mu_1 - \mu_2 = \bar{x}_1 - \bar{x}_2 \pm t(n_1 + n_2 - 2, 0.05) \cdot s \cdot \sqrt{\frac{1}{n_1} + \frac{1}{n_2}}$$

$$= 1.88 \pm 2.306 \cdot 2.115 \cdot \sqrt{\frac{1}{5} + \frac{1}{5}}$$

$$= 1.88 \pm 3.08$$

$$= -1.20 \sim 4.96$$

3) The comparison should be made between specimens as like as possible. To do so, it is better to cut the test-pieces into halves, one half being treated and the other half not. The analysis is carried out to determine whether or not there is any difference within paired specimens.

Index